Anxiety, Inc.

LEONARDO TAVARES

Anxiety, Inc.

ANXIETY, INC.

© Copyright 2023 - Leonardo Tavares

This title may be purchased in bulk for business or educational use.

For information, please email realleotavares@gmail.com.

All rights reserved. No portion of this book may be reproduced, stored in a retrieval system, or transmitted in any form or by any means – electronic, mechanical, photocopy, recording, scanning, or other – except for brief quotations in critical reviews or articles, without the prior written permission of the publisher.

Under no circumstances will any blame or legal responsibility be held against the publisher, or author, for any damages, reparation, or monetary loss due to the information contained within this book, either directly or indirectly.

Legal Notice:

This book is copyright protected. It is only for personal use. You cannot amend, distribute, sell, use, quote or paraphrase any part, or the content within this book, without the consent of the author or publisher.

Disclaimer Notice:

Please note the information contained within this document is for educational and entertainment purpose only. All effort has been executed to present accurate, up to date, reliable, complete information. No warranties of any kind are declared or implied. Readers acknowledge that the author is not engaged in the rendering of legal, financial, medical or professional advice. The content within this book has been derived from various sources. Please consult a licensed professional before attempting any techniques outlined in this book.

By reading this document, the reader agrees that under no circumstances is the author responsible for any losses, direct or indirect that are incurred as a result of the use of the information contained within this document, including but not limited to, errors, omissions, or inaccuracies.

First Printing 2023

CONTENTS

Foreword 9

1. Introduction to the Universe of Anxiety 11
    Understanding Anxiety 12
    The Ubiquity of Anxiety 15
    In Modern Society 15
    An Invitation to Exploration 16

2. A Society in Rapid Transformation 17
    The Impact of Social, Technological, and Cultural Changes on the Rise of Anxiety 18
    Pressures of Modernity Contributing to Stress and Uncertainty . 23

3. Causes of Anxiety 27
    Biological, Genetic, and Environmental Factors 28
    Exploration of Individual and Collective Triggers 31

4. Anxiety and Perfectionism 37
    The Relationship Between the Pursuit of Perfection and Anxiety 38
    Strategies for Dealing with the Need for Perfection and Its Connections to Anxiety 44

5. Mental Health Impacts 51
    Psychological Consequences of Anxiety 52
    How Anxiety Affects Self-Esteem and Confidence 56
    Long-Term Effects of Anxiety on our Mental Health 61
    Strategies to Mitigate the Impacts of Anxiety on Mental Health 75

6. Impacts on Physical Health 104
Effects of Anxiety on Our Body 105
Strategies to Mitigate the Physical Impacts of Anxiety 111

7. The Vicious Cycle of Anxiety 116
Understanding the Self-Perpetuating Cycle of Anxiety............116
Methods to Break the Cycle and Foster Recovery 129

8. Self-Management Strategies 133
Practical Strategies to Face Moments of Heightened Anxiety... 134
Breathing, Relaxation, and Mindfulness Techniques for Anxiety Control 136

9. Building Resilience 144
The Nature of Resilience.. 145
Developing Emotional Resilience.. 145
How to Turn Adversity into Personal Growth 148

10. Lifestyle and Well-Being 159
Strategies to Promote a Healthier, Less Anxious Lifestyle........ 160
The Importance of a Balanced Diet and Physical Exercise in Managing Anxiety 163

11. Technology and Anxiety................................... 167
The Impact of Excessive Technology Use on Anxiety 168
Strategies to Balance Technology Use and Reduce Overload 170

12. Relationships and Social Support 175
The Influence of Relationships on Anxiety 176
Strategies to Cultivate Healthy Relationships and Seek Emotional Support 178

13. Seeking Professional Help 183
The Significance of Seeking Professional Help 184
Demystifying Taboos Surrounding Therapy 186

Conclusion 189
About the Author 191
References 192

FOREWORD

Welcome to "Anxiety, Inc.", an invitation to venture into the intricate corridors of our inner world, where anxiety manifests as an intricate puzzle of emotions, thoughts, and sensations. This is where we begin to unravel the fabric of this universal human experience, offering not only understanding but tangible strategies to tame this emotional whirlwind.

Envision this tome as a guide through the winding paths of anxiety. At times, it's a shadowy labyrinth, yet there is always a glimmer at the end of the tunnel. Here, we seek that light, not only to dispel the shadows of anxiety but also to demystify its enigma.

The journey commences with an analysis of what anxiety truly is, for comprehending our adversary is the initial step towards vanquishing it. We will delve deep into its manifestations, from those nervous jolts to the spiraling thoughts that seem to have a life of their own.

Next, we venture along the paths of anxiety management and control. From age-old breathing techniques to modern mindfulness approaches, we shall explore strategies that offer solace and soothe the heart amidst the tempest.

Yet, it is not merely about surviving anxiety; it is about thriving despite it. Within these pages, you will discover how to transform anxiety into fuel for personal growth. It is an invitation to transcend and grow, facing fears with head held high.

Prepare for this enriching voyage of self-discovery. Embrace the possibility of a lighter and brighter life, where anxiety is no longer a dark shadow but a passing cloud in the vast sky of human existence. We are about to embark on this journey together. Let us explore, learn, and grow. Anxiety shall no longer be a prison but a doorway to liberation.

1
INTRODUCTION TO THE UNIVERSE OF ANXIETY

Open your heart to the universe of anxiety, where each beat unveils a tale of courage and self-discovery.

Anxiety is a universal experience that each one of us, at some juncture in our lives, has encountered. It manifests in various forms and intensities, from daily concerns about responsibilities to that overwhelming sense of apprehension before a significant event. In modern times, anxiety has become a constant companion for many, an unwelcome presence that profoundly and often disabling influenced our lives.

Anxiety is not merely an emotional state; it is a complex and multifaceted response of our organism to perceived threatening or stressful situations. It is a natural and adaptive reaction that readies our body and mind to face challenges. However, when this response becomes excessive, disproportionate, or persistent, it ceases to be beneficial and begins to hinder our quality of life and well-being.

In this chapter, we shall commence our exploration, aiming not only to define and comprehend anxiety in its depth but also to underscore its relevance and prevalence in the intricate webs of modern life. We shall unravel the multifaceted nature of anxiety, revealing its varied and often underestimated manifestations. By grasping its definition and scope, we shall be better equipped to confront the challenges it presents. After all, it is only by understanding the true nature of the adversary that we can forge the necessary weapons to overcome it.

UNDERSTANDING ANXIETY

Anxiety can be described as an emotional state characterized by anticipation, nervousness, and concern regarding the future. It is an emotional and physiological response to a perceived threat, whether real or imagined. The body goes into a state of alert, releasing hormones like adrenaline and cortisol to prepare the organism for action. This response, known as the 'fight or flight response,' is essential for our survival and helps us react to dangerous situations.

However, in certain circumstances, this response can be triggered without a real reason or be disproportionate to the situation. This is where anxiety becomes a problem. When experienced chronically or intensely, anxiety can interfere with our ability to function in daily life, impairing our relationships, work, and overall quality of life.

The Diversity of Anxiety Manifestations

One of the most intriguing characteristics of anxiety is its diversity of manifestations. It is not confined to a single experience or symptom; rather, it presents itself in various ways, each with its nuances and peculiarities. Understanding this diversity is essential to recognize when anxiety is present in our lives.

Excessive Worry: One of the most common manifestations of anxiety is excessive worry. This entails a constant and overwhelming flow of thoughts about future events, even if they are commonplace daily situations. The mind becomes a factory of negative scenarios, and the feeling of apprehension is constant.

Muscle Tension: Another frequent sign of anxiety is muscle tension. Chronic anxiety can lead to stiffness, aches, or physical discomfort due to constant muscle tension. This can manifest as headaches, backaches, and even digestive problems.

Irritability: Anxiety can also influence our emotions, making us more irritable and impatient. Situations that would not normally disturb us can lead to disproportionate reactions due to a constant state of tension.

Restlessness: The sensation of restlessness is another facet of anxiety. It can be difficult to relax, sit calmly, or focus on a specific task. The mind is always racing, and the individual may feel the need to be constantly doing something.

Difficulty Concentrating: Anxiety also affects our ability to concentrate. Staying focused on a task or absorbing information can be challenging when the mind is filled with worries.

Fatigue: Paradoxically, anxiety can cause intense fatigue. Constant physical and emotional tension can drain our energy, leaving us tired and unmotivated, even after a proper night's sleep.

These are just some of the many ways anxiety can manifest. It is important to understand that anxiety is not a uniform experience, and people may experience it differently. It can be a subtle shadow lurking in the background of our lives or an overwhelming storm that engulfs us entirely.

The Ubiquity of Anxiety

To comprehend the relevance of anxiety in contemporary society, it is crucial to acknowledge its omnipresence. Anxiety knows no boundaries, affecting people of all ages, backgrounds, and lifestyles. It makes no distinction based on race, gender, or social status. It is a universal human phenomenon, an intrinsic part of the human experience.

Furthermore, anxiety is not confined to any specific sector of society. It does not discriminate between the affluent and the impoverished, the educated and the uneducated, the urban and the rural. It permeates all spheres of contemporary society, from students concerned about their academic performance to executives under pressure to achieve ambitious goals. Anxiety is, therefore, a concern that cuts across all layers of society.

As a result, anxiety is not only an individual challenge but also a social phenomenon. It shapes our culture, influences our norms, and affects our relationships.

THE UBIQUITY OF ANXIETY IN MODERN SOCIETY

In present times, we dwell in an ever faster and intricate world. The demands of daily life, the pressure for success, the perpetual connectivity through technology, and the uncertainties of the future contribute to a significant surge in anxiety levels. Modern lifestyle often leads us to a state of overwhelm, where the balance between work, leisure, and self-care is frequently neglected.

Modern society imposes upon us a perpetual need to excel, to achieve ambitious goals, and to uphold high standards in all domains of our lives. Social media, while connecting us, can also trigger anxiety through constant comparison with others. We are under scrutiny, assessed, and judged in various ways, round the clock, instilling a growing fear of falling short or not meeting the expectations set upon us.

The pursuit of success, heightened competitiveness, and the quest for perfection are common realities in our modern lives. All these pressures can create a feeding cycle of anxiety, where the need to succeed and the apprehension of not attaining that success generate a state of chronic stress and anxiety.

In this scenario, anxiety often takes on the role of a vexing advisor, an inner voice that questions and urges us to achieve more, to be better, to live up to expectations, both our own and those of others. And thus, anxiety intertwines with the relentless pursuit of success and the persistent avoidance of failure.

AN INVITATION TO EXPLORATION

This book extends an invitation to explore the intricate realm of anxiety, to comprehend its roots, its effects, and its means of control. Throughout the forthcoming chapters, we shall delve into the causes of anxiety, its impacts on mental and physical health, common triggers, and, most importantly, the strategies and techniques that can aid us in facing this challenge positively and effectively.

By offering information, insights, and practical tools, my aim is to empower you to recognize and deal with anxiety in a wholesome manner. Together, let us construct a path towards a balanced life, where anxiety is not a barrier but rather an opportunity for growth and self-development.

2

A SOCIETY IN RAPID TRANSFORMATION

In a world of perpetual change, we find strength in adaptation and wisdom in evolution.

Delving into the core of modernity is akin to engaging in a dizzying dance, an incessant movement where society reinvents itself with each step. We live in an era of sweeping transformations, a whirlwind of changes that sweep through our lives in every dimension. As we witness the ever-evolving landscape, we are challenged to strike a delicate balance between the need for adaptation and the preservation of our mental and emotional well-being. It is on this shifting stage that anxiety emerges as an unwanted partner, a shadow that accompanies us amidst this tumultuous journey.

In this chapter, we invite you to delve deeply into the swift dance of modernity, unraveling the intricate ties between social, technological, and cultural transformations and the escalating spiral of anxiety that this acceleration induces. Each step, each turn in this dance, leaves marks on our collective psyche. It is a choreography that tests the resilience of our mind and the flexibility of our spirit.

Social transformations trigger waves of cultural changes, which in turn find resonance in technological evolution. The internet, social networks, and artificial intelligence shape not only our interactions but also how we perceive reality and even ourselves. However, this frenzied progress comes at a cost, and anxiety becomes a constant echo amidst this advancement. It infiltrates our lives, fueled by uncertainties and the rapid pace of this dance of modernity. Let us learn to dance with modernity, to find harmony between the speed of change and inner peace, and to transform this dizzying dance into a movement of resilience and growth.

THE IMPACT OF SOCIAL, TECHNOLOGICAL, AND CULTURAL CHANGES ON THE RISE OF ANXIETY

The social, technological, and cultural changes that characterize modernity have a profound impact on the increase of anxiety levels in our contemporary society. Let us thoroughly explore each of these dimensions to grasp the complexity of this interplay and its consequences on mental health.

Social Transformations

Society is in a perpetual state of transformation, and social changes stand as one of the main drivers of anxiety. As old structures and norms are challenged and redefined, a sense of uncertainty and instability arises. The revolution in gender roles, diversity, mass migration, and other social phenomena adds an extra layer of complexity to human interactions.

This interplay between individuals and an evolving society can result in anxiety, especially for those who feel lost or overwhelmed by the pace of social changes. The pressure to adapt to new norms and expectations can lead to a sense of inadequacy, contributing to anxiety.

The Technological Revolution

The technological revolution, while providing unprecedented connectivity, also introduces a set of emotional and mental challenges. The extensive use of electronic devices and constant online presence can lead to information overload and a feeling of being always 'connected'.

Moreover, social media creates an environment conducive to constant comparison with others, resulting in an increase in social anxiety. The need to maintain an idealized online image can generate intense pressure to be perceived positively by others, resulting in performance anxiety.

Cultural Changes

Cultural changes are an integral part of the dynamics of modern society, shaping our perceptions, behaviors, and interactions. Contemporary culture is in a perpetual state of evolution, and this transformation has profound implications for how we perceive and live life, which, in turn, influences our mental health.

One striking characteristic of cultural changes is the shift from a collectivist mentality to a more individual-centric culture. Valuing autonomy and the pursuit of personal fulfillment has become a dominant narrative. While this has brought freedom and empowerment, it has also created additional pressure on each individual.

The notion of 'personal achievement' can trigger anxiety as individuals feel pressured to meet high standards and fulfill not only society's expectations but also their own. The relentless pursuit of personal goals and objectives often leads to a constant sense of dissatisfaction and, consequently, anxiety.

Contemporary culture is deeply rooted in the pursuit of consumption and the constant acquisition of new experiences. We live in a society that promotes the idea that acquiring more and seeking new experiences will lead us to happiness and complete satisfaction.

However, this relentless and often unrealistic pursuit of an ideal state of life can generate anxiety. The chronic sense of dissatisfaction arising from the culture of consumption can lead to an anxiety cycle, as we never feel fully content with what we have or have achieved. This can create a constant pressure to acquire more and reach an unattainable standard of 'happiness'.

Cultural changes also influence our interpersonal relationships and our sense of community. We live in an era where relationships are often mediated by technology and physical connections can be replaced by digital interactions. This profoundly impacts our sense of belonging and loneliness.

The redefinition of social ties can lead to anxiety, especially for those who feel disconnected or isolated amidst this transformation. The pressure to maintain an idealized online presence can create a sense of inauthenticity and contribute to social anxiety.

These cultural changes, promoting individuality, consumption, and the redefinition of our relationships, are interconnected and influence our daily experiences. By understanding the role culture plays in modern anxiety, we can develop effective strategies to face this challenge, promoting a more balanced and healthy approach to contemporary life.

Intersection and Connection

The intersection and connection among the dimensions of social, technological, and cultural changes create a complex environment that significantly influences our mental and emotional well-being. This synergy amplifies the effects of these changes, resulting in a cumulative impact on the rise of anxiety in contemporary society.

Social, technological, and cultural transformations are intrinsically intertwined, forming a complex network of influences. Social transformations shape human interactions, and technological innovations directly affect how we communicate, work, and relate. These changes are amplified by cultural evolutions that redefine our values, expectations, and aspirations.

Rapid technological evolution, for instance, directly affects our social interactions. The extensive use of electronic devices and social networks often diminishes the quality and depth of interpersonal relationships, negatively impacting our emotional well-being.

This interconnection and interdependence of modern changes have a cumulative impact on anxiety. The contemporary individual, constantly immersed in this environment of rapid and interconnected changes, often grapples with a state of chronic anxiety.

Understanding this interconnection is fundamental to effectively address anxiety. Coping strategies and interventions must consider the complex interplay among all these aspects. Striking a balance between harnessing the benefits of these changes and mitigating their negative impacts on our mental and emotional health is a challenge.

The pursuit of this balance is crucial to foster a healthier and more sustainable approach to contemporary life. We must learn to use technology consciously, embrace social changes equitably, and constantly question and redefine our cultural values. Only through this balance and an understanding of the interconnection among these dimensions can we address anxiety holistically and strive for a balanced and fulfilling life in the modern era.

PRESSURES OF MODERNITY CONTRIBUTING TO STRESS AND UNCERTAINTY

Modernity has brought forth a host of advancements and benefits to society, yet it has also ushered in unique pressures that can contribute to stress and insecurity in people's lives. Let us delve into these pressures in detail to understand how they affect mental and emotional health in the contemporary world.

One of the most pressing pressures of modernity is the speed at which things change. Technology advances at an exponential pace, social and professional expectations are ever on the rise, and daily life has become incredibly accelerated. This rapid transformation creates a constant need for adaptation and learning, which can generate chronic stress as individuals struggle to keep up.

The growing expectations in all aspects of life, from performance at work to social interactions and the pursuit of personal happiness, can create a constant pressure to meet often unattainable standards, leading to a cycle of stress and anxiety.

We live in the information age, where we are inundated with an unprecedented amount of data and content through the internet and social media. While this offers valuable opportunities, it also generates an information overload. Trying to process and assimilate this constant flow of data can be overwhelming, leading to a state of anxiety and uncertainty about our understanding of the world.

Furthermore, dependence on technology for communication and daily tasks can create a sense of insecurity when we are disconnected or when our privacy is compromised. The fear of being "disconnected" can contribute to anxiety.

Modernity often promotes a culture of constant competition and comparison. In both professional and personal spheres, individuals often find themselves in a relentless race to achieve goals, acquire material possessions, and attain high standards of living. Constant exposure to others' achievements and seemingly ideal lifestyles, amplified by social media, can create pressure to compete and compare, leading to a sense of inadequacy and chronic stress.

This competitive culture can also affect mental health, as individuals constantly feel evaluated by others and society, resulting in an unrelenting search for validation and acceptance.

Modernity often demands extreme dedication to professional life, with long working hours and constant internet connectivity. Striking a balance between professional and personal life can become a challenging endeavor, generating stress due to the pressure to meet demands in both spheres.

The lack of time for leisure activities, self-care, and adequate rest contributes to chronic stress and anxiety. The inability to disconnect from work can lead to a constant state of stress, negatively impacting mental health.

These pressures of modernity are interconnected and pose significant challenges to mental and emotional health. It is crucial to seek a balance between harnessing the advancements and benefits that modernity offers while developing effective strategies to mitigate the stress and insecurity that accompany this fast-paced and demanding lifestyle.

As we conclude this exploration of rapidly transforming society, it becomes clear that we are immersed in an era of dizzying changes. The dance of modernity is complex, challenging, and often overwhelming. Social, technological, and cultural transformations are intrinsically intertwined, creating a scenario that significantly influences our mental and emotional well-being. The pressures of modernity are real, and their ramifications on anxiety are palpable.

However, this chapter also invites us to find the balance between adapting to this frenetic pace and preserving our mental health. By understanding the interconnection of these changes and their cumulative impact, we are in a better position to face the challenges that modernity presents. Our goal now is to explore the roots and foundations of anxiety on a deeper level. It is time to investigate the underlying causes that contribute to this pervasive anxiety in contemporary society.

Stepping into the realm of anxiety, it is imperative to understand the deep-seated roots of this complex phenomenon. Anxiety is not an isolated emotion; it is an echo of diverse influences and experiences that shape our daily lives. The next chapter aims to illuminate the multifaceted causes that trigger and fuel anxiety in our lives. Let us unravel the layers of this complex emotion and discover ways to restore calm and balance amidst this contemporary challenge.

3
CAUSES OF ANXIETY

In the roots of anxiety, we discover the source, but also the seed of triumph.

In the intricate weave of human experience, anxiety emerges as a central piece. It is an emotion that can manifest in diverse ways, from a gentle whisper of apprehension to a deafening roar of terror.

At the core of the causes of anxiety lie the biological mechanisms of our body, where the dance of molecules and electrical signals in the brain dictates our emotional response. Our genes, the building blocks of our existence, also play a role in our propensity for anxiety. However, anxiety is not confined to the depths of biology; it manifests in our psyche, shaped by our past experiences, thought patterns, and personality traits.

Yet, anxiety is not a solitary entity. It is influenced by our environment, by the social tensions of our modern era, and by the lifestyle we choose. Constant stress, relentless social pressures, and the unceasing wave of information in the digital age have become an integral part of our daily lives, playing a vital role in amplifying anxiety. These influences intertwine, creating a dissonant symphony of anxiety in our lives.

As we unravel this complex web of causes, it becomes evident that anxiety is not a mere consequence of our actions or chance; it is an intricate response to a complex set of influences. Anxiety can be seen as an echo of our biology, our social interactions, and our life experiences. It manifests in every aspect of our being, from the circuits of our brain to the scenes of our daily life.

In this chapter, we will uncover each of these causes, explore their nuances, and understand how they contribute to the complex tapestry of anxiety. After all, comprehending the causes is the crucial first step in developing effective coping strategies.

BIOLOGICAL, GENETIC, AND ENVIRONMENTAL FACTORS

Anxiety is a phenomenon resulting from a complex interplay of biological, genetic, and environmental factors. Understanding these influences is essential for developing more effective management and treatment strategies, aiming to address anxiety in a holistic manner. Let's delve deeper into our understanding of each of these fundamental factors.

Biological Factors

Anxiety has a solid biological foundation, with the brain being the epicenter of processing this emotion.

Neurotransmitters such as serotonin, noradrenaline, and GABA play crucial roles. Serotonin, for example, is linked to mood and emotion regulation. Imbalances in these neurotransmitters can lead to a disproportionate anxiogenic response, characteristic of anxiety disorders.

In addition to neurotransmitters, the central nervous system, especially the brain and spinal cord, plays a crucial role in anxiety regulation. Specific parts of the brain, like the amygdala and prefrontal cortex, are particularly involved in anxiety processing and response.

The hormone cortisol, released in response to stress, plays a significant role in the development of anxiety disorders. Chronically elevated levels of cortisol can affect mental health by increasing sensitivity to stress and the likelihood of experiencing anxiety.

Genetic Factors

Anxiety, like many aspects of our health, has an intricate connection with our genetics. Studies reveal that anxiety has a significant genetic basis. Predisposition to anxiety disorders can be genetically inherited, carrying a legacy that influences individual vulnerability. Certain genes play a crucial role in this process, shaping how our brain functions and regulates our emotions.

A family history of anxiety disorders can, therefore, increase the likelihood of someone developing anxiety. Specific genes involved in neurotransmitter regulation, stress response, and emotional regulation can be passed down through generations. These genes shape our reactivity to stressful situations and emotional challenges, directly influencing our susceptibility to anxiety.

Environmental Factors

However, anxiety is not a tale written in genes alone; it is a complex and multifaceted narrative that also takes into account the environment that surrounds us. Our experiences and environmental exposures play a fundamental role in shaping the anxiety we feel.

Being exposed to high-pressure situations, toxic environments, or traumatic events can serve as triggers for anxiety. The impact of the environment cannot be underestimated, as experiences such as trauma, abuse, family instability, violence, or even natural disasters can have profound and lasting effects on our mental health.

Thus, anxiety is a complex interplay between our genetic predisposition and the experiences we undergo. It's like a delicate dance between our genes and the world around us, a dance that shapes each person's unique anxiety experience. Understanding this interconnection helps us approach anxiety in a more holistic and effective manner.

EXPLORATION OF INDIVIDUAL AND COLLECTIVE TRIGGERS

Anxiety, complex and multifaceted, can be triggered by a variety of factors, both at an individual and collective level. These triggers play a fundamental role in the onset and intensity of anxiety symptoms. Let us delve deeply into the individual and collective aspects that contribute to this emotional response.

Individual Triggers

Anxiety, a complex response of the body and mind to external or internal stimuli, can be triggered by various factors. Let us explore in more detail the individual triggers, which originate at a personal level and have a significant impact on the manifestation of anxiety.

Coexisting Mental Health Conditions: Mental health disorders such as depression, bipolar disorder, or post-traumatic stress disorder may intertwine with anxiety. The presence of one condition can exacerbate anxiety and vice versa, creating a complex cycle.

Personality: Certain personality traits, such as excessive perfectionism, excessive shyness, and controlling tendencies, may be associated with a higher risk of developing anxiety disorders.

Traumas and Personal Experiences: Traumas and past experiences are potent triggers for anxiety. Traumatic events, especially in childhood, can create fertile ground for the development of anxiety disorders later in life. These events can leave deep marks on our psyche, leading to an exaggerated anxiety response in similar situations.

Phobias and Specific Fears: Phobias are common triggers for anxiety. Intense and irrational fear of specific situations or objects, such as heights, spiders, flying, among others, can lead to high levels of anxiety when confronted with these elements.

Thinking Style and Cognitive Patterns: The way we think is also a crucial factor. Negative thinking patterns, such as catastrophizing (always anticipating the worst), generalization (extrapolating a negative event to all situations), and polarized thinking (seeing everything as black or white, without middle ground), can contribute to chronic anxiety.

Expectations and Personal Pressures: Pressures to meet personal and social expectations, such as achieving professional goals, maintaining high performance standards, or fulfilling certain social roles, can trigger anxiety. Worry about failure or non-acceptance can be intense.

Negative Thinking Patterns: Dysfunctional thinking patterns, such as catastrophic thinking, always expecting the worst, or anticipating negative outcomes, can continuously trigger anxiety. Negative interpretation of events and experiences can lead to excessive worries and anxieties.

Physical Health Conditions: Physical health conditions, such as heart problems, respiratory issues, or chronic illnesses, can trigger anxiety. Concerns about health and a feeling of lack of control over the body can lead to increased anxiety.

Substance Use: The use of substances such as alcohol, illicit drugs, or certain medications can trigger anxiety. Some substances can affect the brain's chemical balance, leading to anxiety symptoms.

Each person has a unique combination of individual triggers that influence their anxiety. Understanding these factors is vital for effective anxiety management.

Collective Triggers

The collective triggers of anxiety are factors that operate at a social, cultural, or group level, exerting significant influence on the anxiety experienced by a community or society. Let us deepen our understanding of these triggers, highlighting their interconnection with collective mental and emotional health.

Traumatic Social and Cultural Events: The occurrence of traumatic events in a society, such as wars, terrorism, natural disasters, or epidemics, can generate mass anxiety. The uncertainty, fear of the unknown, and a sense of insecurity resulting from these events can trigger widespread anxiety in the population.

Pressures of Modern Society: Modern society, often focused on success, competitiveness, and standards of perfection, can generate anxiety in many individuals. The constant pressure to achieve professional goals, meet social expectations, and maintain an acceptable public image can create an anxious and stressful environment.

Economic Stressors: Economic instability, unemployment, debts, and financial worries affect a significant portion of the population. Uncertainty about financial future and the pressure to sustain a certain standard of living can lead to high levels of anxiety in a community.

Cultural Pressures: Certain cultures may impose specific pressures that contribute to anxiety. Cultural expectations related to marriage, children, gender roles, or professional success can generate anxiety in individuals who feel unable to meet these expectations.

Stigma and Discrimination: Racial, gender, sexual orientation, or social discrimination can cause collective anxiety in marginalized groups. Social stigma and exclusion can create an environment of persistent anxiety in these communities.

Educational Pressures: Competitive educational systems can be significant triggers of anxiety, especially in students. Performance expectations, constant competition, and pressure to succeed academically can lead to high levels of anxiety.

Social and Behavioral Norms: Rigid social norms or behavioral expectations can create anxiety in individuals who do not conform or fear social rejection for being different. The need to fit into certain standards can generate widespread anxiety.

It is crucial to recognize that these factors do not operate in isolation. They are interconnected and can reinforce each other. For example, chronic stress can negatively affect brain neurochemistry, and negative thinking patterns can arise as a result of prolonged stress.

Exposure to Social Media and News: Constant exposure to negative news, disasters, and tragedies through social media and other forms of communication can contribute to collective anxiety. The emotional impact of information overload and constant comparison with others can amplify anxiety.

Collective triggers of anxiety reflect the complex interplay between individuals and society. They illustrate how culture, economy, social norms, and other social factors can influence the mental health of a community. Understanding these social influences is crucial to building a world where anxiety is understood and treated in a holistic and sensitive manner.

In this chapter, we have explored the complexities of the biological, genetic, and environmental factors that contribute to the spiral of anxiety. Now, it is time to direct our attention to one of the most prominent and challenging facets of anxiety in modern society: perfectionism. In the next chapter, we will delve into the universe of perfectionism and unravel how it is intrinsically linked to anxiety and how we can find a healthy balance between the pursuit of excellence and our mental health.

The journey of understanding anxiety continues, with the hope that each step brings us closer to a fulfilling and rewarding life, free from the shackles of anxiety.

4

ANXIETY AND PERFECTIONISM

Challenge perfectionism, celebrate progress, and free yourself from the shackles of endless expectation.

The relentless pursuit of perfection, a quest that winds through the corridors of our ambitions and expectations, is an intricate and often distressing dance that many of us perform in our lives. It is a dance that begins with the noble desire to achieve excellence but can quickly become an emotional trap, entangling us in a relentless cycle of anxiety.

At the heart of this quest lies perfectionism, an attribute that can be both a friend and a foe. In its noblest form, perfectionism can motivate us to seek the best in ourselves, to strive for mastery and enhance our skills. However, in its most challenging form, it becomes an ironclad shirt that stifles self-acceptance, taking us hostage to impossibly high standards and plunging us into an ocean of anxiety.

This chapter is a profound exploration of the interconnection between anxiety and perfectionism. We will unravel the roots of this insatiable desire for perfection and how it often silently precedes the anxiety that haunts us. We will examine the profound origins, the thought patterns that fuel it, and the emotional traps that ensnare us when we relentlessly strive for excellence.

As we delve into this exploration, we will address effective strategies to confront and redirect perfectionism in a healthier manner. We will learn to dance with the pursuit of excellence without losing ourselves in the choreography of anxiety. After all, it is possible to strive for mastery without leaving our mental health behind. It is possible to redefine the meaning of perfection by embracing our humanity and celebrating progress over perfection.

THE RELATIONSHIP BETWEEN THE PURSUIT OF PERFECTION AND ANXIETY

The relationship between the pursuit of perfection and anxiety is a complex and often conflicting interaction between our desires to achieve high standards and the psychological pressure this pursuit places upon us. Let us delve deeper into this relationship, unraveling the psychological mechanisms that fuel it.

Idealization and Internal Pressure

Idealization begins with creating an ideal standard in our minds, often unattainable and unrealistic. We envision the perfect person we want to be, the perfect goals we want to achieve, and the perfect life we want to lead.

This idealized vision creates overwhelming internal pressure. We feel an intense need to achieve these standards at any cost, and this can lead to constant anxiety. The more we strive to attain this imaginary perfection, the more anxious we become. The constant fear of not living up to these unattainable expectations haunts us daily.

This internal pressure can result in various consequences for our mental health. From high levels of stress and anxiety to feelings of inadequacy and low self-esteem. The constant struggle to meet these standards can affect our happiness and satisfaction with life.

To combat this idealization trap and internal pressure, it is vital to develop a more realistic and compassionate perspective about ourselves. This includes accepting our imperfections and understanding that progress is more important than perfection. Learning to value our journeys and accomplishments, however small, is essential to alleviate this relentless pressure and live a more balanced and joyful life.

Fear of Judgment and Social Rejection

Perfectionism often has its roots in the fear of negative judgment from others. In a society where the image we project is highly valued, any deviation from this idealized image is often seen as a failure.

This constant fear of being judged and criticized by others can lead to paralyzing anxiety. The fear of not meeting society's expectations or being seen as less than perfect can prevent us from acting authentically. We may feel an overwhelming pressure to hide our imperfections and insecurities, resulting in a distorted representation of ourselves.

This anxiety regarding social judgment can profoundly impact our mental health. It can lead to a vicious cycle of self-demand, where we strive to meet unattainable standards to avoid the judgment of others. This, in turn, can increase stress and anxiety levels, harming our self-esteem and emotional well-being.

To overcome this paralyzing fear, it is essential to work on accepting our authenticity. This involves valuing our true essence, including our flaws and imperfections, and acknowledging that pleasing everyone is impossible. Developing self-confidence and learning not to overly rely on external validation are crucial steps to break free from the cycle of fear of judgment and social rejection.

Self-Demand

Self-demand is the constant pursuit of perfection, the need to achieve ambitious goals and be impeccable in everything we do. This desire for excellence can turn into a significant source of anxiety.

By setting very high standards, we create constant internal pressure to meet these lofty expectations. We want to be the best, both professionally and personally, and often do not allow ourselves to fail or make mistakes. This self-rigidity can lead to an overwhelming burden of stress and anxiety.

The fear of not reaching our own expectations can become a debilitating source of anxiety. We feel constant pressure to be perfect, and when we do not achieve this ideal, we can feel inadequate and insufficient. This cycle of self-demand and anxiety can be highly detrimental to our mental health.

To deal with self-demand and its impact on anxiety, it is essential to reassess and readjust our expectations. We need to learn to be compassionate with ourselves, accepting that we are human and, therefore, susceptible to flaws and imperfections. It is important to set realistic and achievable goals, recognizing that progress is more important than perfection.

Furthermore, developing a growth mindset, where we view challenges as opportunities for learning and growth, can help us deal with self-demand in a healthier way. Seeking support from a mental health professional can also be crucial in learning effective strategies to manage self-demand and reduce the associated anxiety.

Comparison and Unbridled Competition

Constant comparison with others and unbridled competition can have significant effects on our mental and emotional well-being. The digital era and the proliferation of social networks have brought a new landscape where people share their achievements, travels, professional accomplishments, and positive aspects of their lives publicly. Constant exposure to this information can create a sense of pressure for us to also meet these standards or surpass others' accomplishments.

The act of comparing ourselves with others is natural and, in many cases, can serve as a drive to strive for and achieve our goals. However, when this comparison becomes obsessive and constant, it can lead to high levels of anxiety and stress. We measure our own worth and success by the standards we see in others, often forgetting that each person has their unique journey and circumstances.

Unbridled competition stems from this constant comparison, where we feel the need not only to keep up with others but to outperform them. This can result in a cycle of overexertion, anxiety, and at times, emotional exhaustion. The need to stand out and be perceived as successful in society can contribute to a constant sense of inadequacy and anxiety.

To deal with this pattern, it is essential to practice awareness and acceptance that each person has their own journey and challenges. It is important to recognize that others' achievements do not diminish our own. Focusing on realistic personal goals and valuing individual progress can help alleviate the pressure of comparison and unbridled competition.

Furthermore, limiting exposure to social media and cultivating a mindset of gratitude for what we have achieved can contribute to a greater emotional balance. Seeking support from a mental health professional can also be useful to develop effective strategies to deal with the anxiety generated by this constant comparison and unbridled competition in today's society.

A Sense of Lack of Control

The pursuit of perfection is often rooted in the illusory belief that if we can control every variable in our lives and achieve ideal standards, we will have a perfectly controlled life. The mistaken perception is that by attaining this perfection, we will be immune to setbacks, failures, or unpredictable situations.

However, the reality is that we cannot control every aspect of life. Life is inherently uncertain and imperfect. Unexpected events, changing circumstances, and unforeseen challenges are an integral part of human existence. The sense of lack of control arises when we perceive the inevitability and unpredictability of life, even when we are committed to achieving perfection.

This unrestrained pursuit of perfection is often an attempt to compensate for this perceived lack of control. We erroneously believe that by reaching a state of perfection in different areas of our lives, we can master all eventualities and ensure that everything goes according to plan. This illusion creates an unbearable pressure to meet unattainable standards.

The feeling of lack of control, fueled by the pursuit of perfection, can lead to high levels of anxiety. The fear of losing control, of not meeting the established standards, and facing failures can become debilitating. Anxiety arises from the constant attempt to anticipate and mitigate all possible setbacks, which is impossible to do in a complex and unpredictable world.

Dealing with this sense of lack of control requires a shift in mindset. It is important to accept the unpredictable nature of life and learn to tolerate uncertainty. Accepting that we cannot control everything is a crucial step in alleviating the anxiety associated with the pursuit of perfection. Learning to adapt and deal with the unexpected in a healthy and balanced way can promote better mental and emotional health.

The interaction between the pursuit of perfection and anxiety is a cycle of high expectations, constant fear of failure, self-demand, incessant comparison, and a feeling that it is never enough. It is crucial to recognize that perfection is an unattainable mirage and instead strive for excellence, progress, and authenticity. Accepting our imperfections and valuing the journey is a crucial step in alleviating the anxiety that arises from this tireless quest for perfection.

STRATEGIES FOR DEALING WITH THE NEED FOR PERFECTION AND ITS CONNECTIONS TO ANXIETY

Dealing with the need for perfection and its connections to anxiety is a challenging process, yet fundamental to promoting mental and emotional well-being. Let's explore practical and effective strategies to confront this pattern of perfectionism and alleviate the associated anxiety.

Identification and Awareness

The initial step is to acknowledge that you are trapped in the cycle of perfectionism and the anxiety it generates. Be conscious of the rigid standards you impose upon yourself and the pressures to be flawless in all aspects of life. Self-awareness is the crucial starting point for change.

Embracing Imperfection Acceptance

Accepting that perfection is an unrealistic goal and that making mistakes is natural is the first step in alleviating the anxiety associated with perfectionism. Embracing our imperfections allows us to live with less pressure and constant judgment. Here are some additional considerations:

Shared Humanity: Remember that everyone, without exception, makes mistakes and faces challenges. Imperfection is part of the human experience. Recognizing this can help reduce the pressure to be perfect.

Reframing Mistakes: Instead of viewing mistakes as failures, see them as opportunities for growth. Each mistake contains valuable lessons that can enhance your future performance.

Practicing Self-Compassion

Rather than punishing ourselves for errors or failures, we must learn to treat ourselves with the same compassion and kindness we would offer to a dear friend. Self-compassion helps us move away from the relentless self-demanding anxiety. Here are some additional insights:

Self-Empathy: Cultivating self-empathy involves speaking to yourself in the same way you would to a dear friend during challenging times. Instead of harsh criticism, offer yourself words of encouragement and support.

Kind Treatment: Remember that you deserve to be treated kindly and respectfully, regardless of your performance or achievements. Nurturing a healthy relationship with yourself is essential for reducing anxiety.

Focusing on the Process, Not Just the Outcome

Rather than obsessively focusing solely on the end result and standards of perfection, it's important to value the process. Appreciating each step and learning from experiences can reduce the anxiety associated with the desire for perfection.

Growth Mindset: Adopt a growth mindset, which focuses on continuous learning and personal development. This helps reduce the pressure to achieve immediate and perfect results.

Celebrating Small Victories: By celebrating small victories and milestones along the way, you acknowledge progress, maintain motivation, and reduce anxiety related to the final outcome.

Setting Realistic and Attainable Goals

It is vital to set realistic goals, taking into account our abilities and circumstances. Achievable goals allow us to progress in a healthy and realistic manner, reducing anxiety related to irrational self-demand.

SMART Goals: Consider using the SMART method (Specific, Measurable, Achievable, Relevant, and Time-bound) to set clear, attainable goals tailored to your reality.

Regular Evaluation: Periodically assess your goals to ensure they remain realistic and relevant, making adjustments as necessary.

Learning from Mistakes

See mistakes and failures as learning opportunities. Instead of despairing when you make a mistake, objectively analyze it, identify what you can learn from it, and apply these lessons in the future. This approach helps reduce anxiety related to the fear of failure.

Constructive Self-Reflection: Deepen your understanding of errors by seeking patterns and ways to improve.

Implementation of Improvements: Turn learning into action by adjusting your approaches to achieve more effective performance.

Establishing Healthy Boundaries

Learn to set realistic boundaries for yourself. Recognize your capabilities and know when it's time to rest and take care of yourself. Don't overwhelm yourself with excessive expectations and endless tasks. Establishing healthy boundaries can help alleviate anxiety stemming from constant pressure.

Prioritization: Identify your priorities and focus on them. Learn to say no to commitments that do not contribute to your well-being.

Time for Self-Care: Set aside time regularly to nurture yourself, be it through relaxing activities, exercise, or hobbies that bring you joy.

Seeking Professional Assistance

If perfectionism and anxiety persist, consider seeking the help of a mental health professional. Specialized therapists can offer specific techniques, such as cognitive-behavioral therapy (CBT), to address perfectionism and its connections to anxiety.

Therapeutic Partnership: Collaborate with a therapist to understand and overcome perfectionistic standards, promoting healing and growth.

Practicing Mindfulness and Relaxation

Engaging in mindfulness and relaxation techniques, such as mindful breathing and meditation, can help reduce the anxiety associated with the need to be perfect.

By focusing on the present and calming the mind, you can alleviate the pressure of perfectionism.

Regular Exercises: Dedicate time daily to mindfulness exercises, like meditation, mindful breathing, or yoga. This will help calm the mind and reduce anxiety.

Integration into Daily Life: In addition to formal mindfulness sessions, practice mindfulness in everyday situations. Be present in the moment, rather than worrying about perfection or future outcomes.

Celebrating Progress

Learn to celebrate progress, not just the end result. Applaud yourself for every small achievement and acknowledge your efforts. This helps maintain a positive perspective and reduce anxiety related to the pursuit of perfection.

Symbolic Rewards: Create rewards or rituals to celebrate your achievements, however small. This reinforces a sense of accomplishment and encourages ongoing progress.

Daily Gratitude: Practice gratitude by recognizing things you are grateful for daily. This helps cultivate a positive mindset.

The relentless pursuit of perfection is an exhausting journey, an emotional maze that often entraps us in unattainable expectations. Perfectionism, with its deep roots in the desire to be flawless, excessive self-demand, and persistent fear of failure, is a significant source of anxiety in our lives. This anxiety, fueled by an unrelenting desire for perfection, can erode our mental health, undermine our self-esteem, and leave us anxious about others' relentless evaluation.

In the next chapter, we will delve into the territory of the impacts of anxiety on our mental health. We will explore how anxiety affects our minds, emotions, and overall well-being. Understanding the ramifications of this complex interplay is a significant step towards cultivating a healthier relationship with our own expectations, seeking a balance between the pursuit of excellence and loving acceptance of our imperfections.

5

MENTAL HEALTH IMPACTS

The mind is resilient; uncover its strength and transform anxiety into empowerment.

Anxiety is an intricate maze of emotions and thoughts that, when uncontrolled, can have significant effects on our mental health. It is a natural and adaptive response to stressful situations, preparing us to deal with imminent challenges. However, when anxiety becomes chronic, exceeding healthy bounds, it turns into an obstacle that can impair the quality of life, affect our cognition, disrupt our emotions, and impact even our relationships.

This chapter aims to delve into the intricacies of this complex relationship between anxiety and mental health. Together, we will explore the profound and often insidious effects anxiety can have on our psychological well-being in the short and long term. Understanding the nature of these impacts is vital for us to seek appropriate treatments and coping strategies.

In this context, this chapter seeks not only to educate about the impacts of anxiety on mental health but also to highlight strategies and techniques that can assist in mitigating these adverse effects. Having an arsenal of tools that allows us to confront anxiety is fundamental for a balanced and productive life.

PSYCHOLOGICAL CONSEQUENCES OF ANXIETY

Anxiety is a universal experience, a natural response of the human body to stress and perceived threats. However, when this response becomes chronic or excessive, it can trigger a series of significant psychological consequences. Let's explore the implications of anxiety for mental health, examining anxiety disorders, the relationship with depression and burnout, as well as its impact on self-esteem and confidence.

Anxiety Disorders

Anxiety itself is not pathological; in fact, it is an essential part of the human experience. However, when anxiety becomes intense and persistent, it can evolve into clinically significant anxiety disorders. Anxiety disorders are characterized by excessive worries and fears, accompanied by physical and psychological symptoms.

Generalized Anxiety Disorder (GAD): People with GAD experience chronic anxiety and constant worry about various aspects of life, such as work, health, family, and relationships. These concerns are difficult to control and can lead to physical symptoms like muscle tension and insomnia.

Panic Disorder: Panic disorder is marked by sudden and intense bouts of anxiety, known as panic attacks. These episodes can be so terrifying that the person may fear having another attack, leading to a cycle of constant anxiety.

Post-Traumatic Stress Disorder (PTSD): PTSD occurs after exposure to traumatic events, such as accidents, abuse, or violent situations. Symptoms include nightmares, flashbacks, and hypervigilance, along with intense anxiety.

Phobias: Phobias are intense and irrational fears of specific objects, situations, or animals. Exposure to these triggers triggers extreme anxiety, leading to avoiding these situations at all costs.

Obsessive-Compulsive Disorder (OCD): OCD is characterized by intrusive and unwanted thoughts (obsessions) that lead to repetitive behaviors and rituals (compulsions) intended to relieve anxiety. These actions can consume a lot of time and energy.

Social Anxiety Disorder (Social Phobia): Social phobia involves an intense fear of judgment or humiliation in social situations. This can lead to avoiding social interactions, which can have a significant impact on personal and professional life.

Depression and Anxiety

The relationship between anxiety and depression is complex and often bidirectional. Many people with anxiety disorders also experience depressive symptoms, and vice versa. This is known as comorbidity, where two or more mental health conditions coexist in a person.

Anxiety and depression share common symptoms such as difficulty sleeping, fatigue, irritability, and difficulty concentrating. These overlaps can make diagnosis and treatment more challenging. When anxiety and depression occur together, they can be more debilitating than when each occurs in isolation.

Excessive worry and rumination, characteristic of anxiety, can lead to negative thoughts and pessimism, contributing to depressive symptoms. Moreover, the social isolation resulting from anxiety can increase the risk of developing depression.

Burnout Syndrome

Burnout syndrome is a state of physical and emotional exhaustion due to chronic stress, often related to work. While it is not an anxiety disorder per se, there is significant overlap between anxiety and burnout. People with burnout often experience anxiety due to overload and constant pressure.

Burnout symptoms include exhaustion, cynicism towards work, reduced performance, and physical symptoms such as headaches and insomnia. Anxiety can arise as a response to prolonged stress associated with burnout, leading to an overwhelming sense of overwhelm.

Destructive Cycle: Anxiety, Depression, and Burnout

These conditions—anxiety, depression, and burnout—can create a destructive cycle. Anxiety can lead to exhaustion and chronic fatigue, triggering or exacerbating depressive symptoms. In turn, depression can heighten anxiety, creating a cycle that weakens mental and physical health.

This cycle can make daily activities challenging and undermine a person's quality of life. Work responsibilities, social interactions, and even the simplest tasks can seem overwhelming, leading to a downward spiral of worsening mental state.

Given this intricate interconnection between anxiety, depression, and burnout, seeking professional help for accurate diagnosis and appropriate treatment is crucial. An integrated treatment plan that addresses not only the symptoms but also the underlying causes can be highly effective.

Cognitive-behavioral therapies (CBT) are often used to treat anxiety and depression disorders. They help individuals identify and modify negative thought patterns and dysfunctional behaviors, promoting healthy coping skills.

Moreover, stress management strategies, relaxation practices, lifestyle changes, and emotional support are essential components of treatment. Engaging in activities that bring pleasure and meaning, such as hobbies or social activities, can also contribute to recovery.

HOW ANXIETY AFFECTS SELF-ESTEEM AND CONFIDENCE

The relationship between anxiety, self-esteem, and confidence is a complex web of psychological interactions that shape our perception of ourselves and our place in the world. Anxiety can have a profound and lasting impact on self-esteem and confidence, affecting how we view ourselves and our relationships with others. Let us delve more deeply into how anxiety affects these crucial aspects of our mental health and well-being.

Excessive Self-Criticism and Erosion of Self-Esteem

Anxiety creates a fertile ground for relentless self-criticism. We live constantly in a heightened state of alert, evaluating every action, word, or decision we make, searching for any sign of failure or inadequacy. This pattern of constant self-criticism gradually undermines our self-esteem, becoming a cruel inner voice that amplifies every mistake, no matter how small, turning them into evidence of our supposed incompetence.

Constant self-criticism and the resulting erosion of self-esteem have a profound impact on all areas of our lives. It affects our performance at work, undermining confidence in our abilities and competencies. In personal relationships, low self-esteem can create barriers to intimacy and genuine connection. This erosion of self-esteem extends to our view of ourselves, shaping our identities and our sense of self-worth.

The journey to overcome self-criticism is a journey towards self-acceptance, self-love, and building a healthy self-esteem. It is a crucial step to enjoy a fulfilling and rewarding life.

Insecurity: The Seed of Doubt

Anxiety often finds its origins in insecurity, an insidious seed of doubt planted deep in our psyche. The persistent feeling of not being good enough or not possessing the necessary capabilities to face life's challenges is the fertile ground for anxiety to thrive. Let us explore this theme and its implications further.

Insecurity can stem from various sources, such as past experiences of failure, rejection, trauma, strict upbringing, or unattainable social standards. These experiences shape our perception of ourselves and the world around us, leading us to doubt our competence.

This insecurity, when left unaddressed, feeds anxiety. Even when we achieve success and receive external validation, the insecurity persists, creating a harmful cycle. Anxiety makes us fear that others will discover our supposed inadequacy, generating more insecurity and anxiety.

Insecurity undermines our confidence in our abilities and competencies. It prevents us from taking risks and challenging ourselves, limiting our personal and professional growth. This lack of self-confidence can sabotage relationships, careers, and life goals, leading to impaired self-esteem.

Overcoming insecurity is an essential step to break the cycle of anxiety. By cultivating a positive mindset and learning to trust our abilities, we can not only alleviate anxiety but also lead a more fulfilling and rewarding life.

Fear of Judgment and the Imprisonment of Inauthenticity

Social anxiety is a significant challenge for many individuals, where the fear of others' judgment becomes a daily reality. In this context, social interactions, something that should be natural and comfortable, become intense sources of stress. Let us delve deeper into this dynamic and how it affects our authenticity and self-esteem.

Social anxiety often has deep roots in past experiences, trauma, bullying, or even lack of social experience. It can manifest as a fear of public speaking, interacting in meetings, or even in more informal social situations.

Fear of judgment from others creates a vicious cycle. It begins with anxious anticipation of a social interaction, followed by intense fear during the interaction, and often culminates in post-event overanalysis, where we reevaluate every detail of the interaction, often in a negative way.

This constant fear of judgment leads us to create masks and facades to protect ourselves. Instead of being authentic and expressing who we really are, we play a role to avoid judgment. This erodes our self-esteem, as we are constantly living a distorted version of ourselves.

Overcoming the fear of judgment requires time, patience, and continuous effort. By working on accepting who we are, challenging our fears, and seeking support when needed, we can free ourselves from the imprisonment of inauthenticity and live more genuinely, enhancing our self-esteem and emotional well-being.

Avoiding Challenges and Erosion of Confidence

Anxiety often leads us to avoid situations that we perceive as challenging or uncomfortable. While this avoidance provides temporary relief from discomfort, in the long run, it undermines our self-confidence and inhibits our personal development. Let us delve into this dynamic and explore strategies to overcome the cycle of avoiding challenges.

Avoidance is a common strategy to cope with anxiety. It is a natural reaction to avoid the emotional discomfort that challenging situations can bring. However, this constant avoidance prevents us from facing and overcoming our fears and challenges.

By avoiding challenges, we miss valuable opportunities for personal and professional growth. This contributes to the erosion of self-confidence, as we never face and overcome these obstacles to prove to ourselves our ability to deal with them.

Avoidance creates a harmful cycle. We avoid a challenging situation, which brings us temporary relief from anxiety. However, this avoidance reinforces our belief that we are not capable of facing that situation, further undermining our self-confidence.

Avoiding challenges, while it may provide temporary comfort, has a long-term cost to our self-confidence and personal growth. By facing our fears and challenges head-on, even gradually, we can rebuild our self-confidence, learn, and grow. Keep in mind that it is through challenges that we grow and become the best version of ourselves.

Catastrophic Thoughts and the Shattering of Self-Esteem

Anxiety is often intertwined with a negative and distorted mental narrative, resulting in catastrophic thoughts. These exaggerated and overly negative thoughts anticipate the worst outcomes in various situations, leading to a degradation of self-esteem. Let us delve more deeply into this dynamic and explore ways to reverse this pattern.

Catastrophic thoughts are cognitive distortions that amplify the negative side of circumstances and minimize the positive. They tend to be irrational, exaggerated, and not based on actual facts.

These constant thoughts of disaster undermine our self-esteem, convincing us of our supposed inability to overcome the challenges we face. By convincing us that the worst is always about to happen, we lose confidence in our abilities and competencies.

Catastrophic thoughts trigger a cascade of anxiety and fear, leading to more negative thoughts and detrimental self-evaluation. This forms a vicious cycle that affects how we perceive ourselves and our potential.

Catastrophic thoughts are like shackles that bind our self-esteem and self-confidence. Challenging them and cultivating a positive attitude can help rebuild our self-image and empower us to face life's challenges with courage and resilience. Remember, you are stronger than your negative thoughts.

LONG-TERM EFFECTS OF ANXIETY ON OUR MENTAL HEALTH

Anxiety, when persistent and unmanaged over time, can result in a myriad of significant impacts on our mental health. These long-term effects can alter our quality of life, daily functioning, and interpersonal relationships, manifesting in various ways:

Chronic Anxiety Disorders

Anxiety, when persistent and unmanaged over time, can evolve into a range of chronic anxiety disorders, each with its own characteristics and impacts on daily life. These disorders can be truly debilitating, affecting both the quality of life and the ability to fully enjoy experiences and social interactions.

Generalized Anxiety Disorder (GAD): This disorder is characterized by chronic and excessive worries about various everyday life situations. Individuals with GAD often struggle to control their worries and may experience constant anxiety even when there is no imminent threat. This can negatively impact their performance at work, interpersonal relationships, and physical health.

Panic Disorder: People with panic disorder experience sudden and intense panic attacks, accompanied by an overwhelming sense of fear and terror, even when there is no real threat. These attacks can lead to persistent worry about when the next attack will occur, resulting in avoidance of places or situations where the attacks may happen.

Post-Traumatic Stress Disorder (PTSD): PTSD is a prolonged and intense response to a traumatic event, such as abuse, accidents, or combat experiences. Symptoms include flashbacks, nightmares, hypervigilance, and avoidance of trauma-related triggers. This can have a profound impact on quality of life and the ability to engage in daily activities.

Specific Phobias: Phobias are intense and irrational fears of specific objects, animals, situations, or activities. These fears can be so debilitating that they lead to extreme avoidance of the feared object or situation, interfering with daily activities and overall happiness.

Obsessive-Compulsive Disorder (OCD): OCD is characterized by obsessions, repetitive and unwanted thoughts, often accompanied by compulsive behaviors to relieve the anxiety generated by the obsessions. These compulsive rituals can consume a lot of time and interfere with daily functioning.

These chronic anxiety disorders not only affect mental health but also have a considerable impact on daily functioning and social interactions. It is crucial to seek professional help for assessment, accurate diagnosis, and treatment, which may include therapy, medication, and coping strategies to effectively manage these disorders and enhance the quality of life. Awareness of these disorders is essential to reduce stigma and encourage those suffering to seek help and support.

Depression

Prolonged anxiety not only bears the burden of its own distress but can also trigger or intensify depression, a severe mental condition that broadly affects our emotional, cognitive, and behavioral life.

Onset and Progression: Chronic anxiety can serve as fertile ground for the development of depression. Constant worry, a sense of helplessness, and incessant apprehension can gradually undermine our emotional resilience, leading to persistent sadness and hopelessness.

Amplified Symptoms: The simultaneous presence of anxiety and depression often amplifies the symptoms of both conditions. The intrusive thoughts and excessive worries of anxiety blend with deep sadness, leading to an overwhelming emotional burden. Physical and mental exhaustion also becomes more pronounced.

Hopelessness and Helplessness: Prolonged anxiety can erode our ability to see a light at the end of the tunnel. The relentless battle against anxiety can leave us feeling there's no way out, contributing to hopelessness, a key component of depression.

Isolation and Withdrawal: Anxiety can lead us to withdraw from the world, avoiding social situations and even daily activities. This social withdrawal can deepen feelings of loneliness and helplessness, thus fueling depression.

Difficulties in Daily Functioning: Combined anxiety and depression can impair our ability to function effectively at work, school, or in our daily responsibilities. Lack of concentration, fatigue, and a sense of emotional overwhelm become significant obstacles.

Treatment Response: Treating depression in individuals also dealing with anxiety can be more complex. Often, treatment needs to address both anxiety and depression in an integrated manner, using therapy and, in some cases, medication.

Importance of Support: Social and emotional support is crucial for individuals facing this dual battle. Having a comprehensive and supportive support network can make a significant difference in the recovery process.

It is essential to understand that depression triggered by prolonged anxiety is not a sign of weakness or personal failure. Seeking help from a mental health professional is vital to obtain the correct diagnosis and a comprehensive treatment plan. Awareness and understanding of these complex interactions between anxiety and depression are crucial to promote compassion and empathy, as well as to develop effective prevention and early intervention strategies.

Social Isolation

Social isolation, often triggered by chronic anxiety, sets off a cycle of negative impacts that significantly affect both our mental health and quality of life.

Origin of Isolation: Chronic anxiety can lead us to retreat from social interactions. Social situations may be perceived as threatening, prompting us to avoid social events, encounters with people, or even everyday activities. This avoidance behavior is an attempt to escape the discomfort that social anxiety brings.

Avoidance and Reduced Opportunities: Prolonged and constant avoidance of social interactions can reduce our opportunities for growth, learning, and meaningful connections. Social interactions are crucial for our personal and emotional development, and isolation can deprive us of these opportunities.

Exacerbation of Anxiety: Isolation can exacerbate our anxiety, creating a vicious cycle. Loneliness can heighten our feelings of inadequacy and reinforce the belief that we are incapable of social interaction. This, in turn, amplifies anxiety when facing new social situations.

Threatened Mental Health: Prolonged isolation can lead to a significant decline in our mental health. Loneliness can trigger feelings of sadness, depression, and despair, negatively impacting our emotional well-being.

Difficulty in Forming Relationships: Social isolation can impair our ability to form and maintain healthy relationships. Lack of practice in social interactions can leave us uncomfortable in social situations, making it harder to establish meaningful connections.

Breaking the Cycle: To break the cycle, it is crucial to seek professional support and help. Therapists can provide strategies to overcome social anxiety and gradually reintegrate into social life. Additionally, participating in support groups can provide a sense of community and understanding.

Strategies for Social Reintegration: Starting with small social interactions and gradually expanding them can aid in social reintegration. Setting realistic goals and celebrating progress, no matter how small, is essential to gain confidence.

Building a Support Network: Investing in meaningful relationships with friends, family, or groups with common interests can be a way to break the cycle of isolation. Sharing our experiences and emotions with others can alleviate anxiety.

Social isolation is a serious and complex challenge, and recognizing its relationship with anxiety is a crucial step in finding effective solutions. Seeking professional support and adopting gradual strategies for social reintegration can help rebuild our confidence and establish meaningful social connections.

Concentration and Memory Challenges

Chronic anxiety, with its incessant mental activity and ceaseless worries, can have deleterious effects on our ability to concentrate and remember, impacting various facets of our lives.

Mental Overload and its Ramifications: Chronic anxiety can lead to constant mental overload. Persistent worries and intrusive thoughts can make it difficult to maintain focus on a specific task. This mental overload compromises our ability to concentrate effectively.

Anxiety and Cognitive Performance: Chronic anxiety can adversely affect cognitive performance. The ability to process information, reason, learn, and recall can be impaired when our minds are constantly consumed by worries and anxieties.

Impact on Daily Activities: Difficulty in focus and ineffective memory can impact our daily activities, from simple tasks to professional and academic commitments. This can lead to a sense of inadequacy and frustration, further heightening anxiety.

Effect on Work and Study Productivity: In the workplace or academic environment, chronic anxiety can impair our productivity. The ability to focus on specific tasks and retain essential information can be compromised, impacting our results and performance.

Interference in Relationships: Lack of focus and memory lapses can interfere with relationships. Forgetting important dates, commitments, or details can lead to misunderstandings and conflicts, affecting the quality of our personal and professional relationships.

Seeking Solutions: To combat these issues, it is essential to manage anxiety effectively. Stress-reduction practices, such as meditation and breathing exercises, can help calm the mind and enhance concentration. Additionally, cognitive-behavioral therapy (CBT) can be an effective approach to address anxiety and its cognitive effects.

Healthy Habits: Maintaining healthy habits, such as a balanced diet, regular physical exercise, and adequate sleep, can enhance our cognitive ability. These habits contribute to mental and physical health, aiding in anxiety reduction and improving concentration and memory.

Time Management and Organization: Developing time management and organizational skills can help deal with mental overload. Establishing priorities, creating task lists, and breaking down large projects into smaller parts can facilitate concentration and effective task completion.

Chronic anxiety can have detrimental effects on our ability to concentrate and remember, impacting the quality of our daily life, academic and professional performance, as well as our personal relationships. An effective approach to anxiety management can help mitigate these impacts and enhance our cognitive function.

Irritability and Mood Swings

Prolonged anxiety affects not only our mind but also our emotions and behaviors, often resulting in irritability and frequent mood swings. These emotional aspects are reflections of the constant state of alertness and tension we experience when dealing with chronic anxiety.

Amplified Reactions: Anxiety can lead to heightened emotional reactions. Stressful situations we would normally manage can trigger disproportionate responses, resulting in bursts of anger, frustration, and intensified irritation.

Reduced Frustration Tolerance: Due to mental overload, anxious individuals often have a lower tolerance for frustration. Everyday situations that don't go as planned or encounter obstacles can result in heightened irritation and impatience.

Vicious Cycle: Irritability resulting from anxiety can, in turn, feed more anxiety. Feeling constantly overwhelmed and irritable can lead to more worries and stress, creating a vicious cycle that is challenging to break.

Impact on Interpersonal Relationships: These mood swings and irritability can negatively impact our relationships. Family, friends, and colleagues may struggle to cope with our emotional fluctuations, which can harm the quality of our relationships.

Self-Criticism and Guilt: After episodes of irritability, individuals with chronic anxiety often experience intensified self-criticism and feelings of guilt. They may blame themselves for not being able to control their emotions or for causing discomfort to others.

The Importance of Self-Reflection: It is crucial for anxious individuals to practice self-reflection to understand their emotional and behavioral reactions. Identifying patterns of irritability and triggers can help develop effective anxiety management strategies.

Relaxation Techniques and Calm Response: Incorporating relaxation techniques such as meditation, deep breathing, and muscle relaxation exercises can help calm the mind and reduce irritability. Learning to respond in a calmer and controlled manner to stressful situations is essential.

Open Communication: Openly communicating with close individuals about anxiety and its effects can help build understanding and support. Explaining that irritability is a symptom of anxiety, not a reflection of displeasure towards them, is crucial.

Dealing with irritability and frequent mood swings caused by anxiety is a challenge, but it is possible with effective coping strategies. Awareness of these emotional reactions and seeking professional help when needed are important steps to improve the quality of life and relationships.

Substance Abuse

Substance abuse is a serious issue often intertwined with chronic anxiety. Individuals facing prolonged anxiety may resort to the use of alcohol, illicit drugs, improperly prescribed medications, or other substances as a way to cope with their symptoms. Unfortunately, this form of self-medication leads to a harmful vicious cycle that worsens both anxiety and substance abuse.

Self-Medication and Temporary Relief: Self-medication is a coping mechanism where a person seeks immediate relief from anxiety symptoms through the use of psychoactive substances. Alcohol and drugs can provide temporary relief from anxiety, leading to their repetition as a coping strategy.

Exacerbation of Anxiety: While substances may initially alleviate anxiety, their prolonged use can lead to worsening anxiety symptoms. Tolerance can develop, necessitating larger doses to achieve the same effect, resulting in a cycle of dependence and escalating anxiety.

Physical and Mental Consequences: Substance abuse can cause significant physical and mental harm, exacerbating anxiety symptoms. This includes health problems, cognitive impairment, mood changes, and other adverse effects.

Guilt and Shame: The cycle of substance abuse and anxiety can lead to intense feelings of guilt, shame, and compromised self-esteem. The individual may feel helpless to break this cycle and face the negative consequences of their behavior.

Intervention and Treatment: Breaking the cycle of substance abuse and anxiety requires professional intervention. Treatment programs addressing both chemical dependency and anxiety are essential. This can include cognitive-behavioral therapy, counseling, support groups, and, in some cases, medication.

Social Support and Support Network: Having a strong and encouraging support network is crucial to breaking the cycle of substance abuse and anxiety. Friends, family, or support groups can provide emotional and practical support during the recovery process.

Development of Alternative Coping Strategies: It is crucial to learn alternative coping strategies for anxiety that do not involve substance use. This can include relaxation techniques, physical exercise, meditation, mindfulness, and therapies.

Awareness of Risks: Raising awareness about the risks associated with substance abuse in managing anxiety is important. Educating individuals about the detrimental effects of this practice can help prevent the cycle of self-medication.

Breaking the cycle of substance abuse and anxiety is a vital step towards recovery and well-being. Seeking professional help and relying on the support of loved ones are essential steps to overcome this challenge and achieve a balanced and healthy life.

Suicidal Thoughts and Self-Harm

Untreated and neglected chronic anxiety can unravel into a dire outcome where affected individuals may grapple with suicidal thoughts or engage in self-harm. This state is a devastating result of the persistence of overwhelming anxiety, leading to an extreme sense of despair and helplessness.

Suicidal Ideations: Chronic anxiety can culminate in suicidal thoughts, wherein the afflicted person feels that the only way to escape their suffering is to end their own life. This stage is critical and demands immediate intervention and professional support.

Profound Hopelessness: The sense of despair associated with untreated chronic anxiety is intense and overwhelming. Individuals may feel trapped in an endless cycle of anxiety, perceiving no hope for improvement.

Isolation and Solitude: Those struggling with suicidal thoughts often experience profound isolation and loneliness in their pain. Chronic anxiety can lead to social isolation, further exacerbating the feelings of solitude and helplessness.

Self-Harm as a Coping Mechanism: In an attempt to alleviate emotional pain, some individuals may resort to self-harm. Cutting or inflicting physical pain can temporarily distract from the extreme emotional agony, but it is an exceedingly harmful strategy.

Desperate Quest for Relief: Suicidal thoughts and self-harm often stem from a desperate quest for relief from intense emotional suffering. People may feel so overwhelmed that death or self-harm seems to be their only escape options.

Importance of Immediate Intervention: Early detection of these signs is crucial for effective intervention. Friends, family, and healthcare professionals need to be vigilant for any indications of suicidal thoughts and act promptly, directing the individual to specialized help.

Specialized Treatment and Ongoing Support: Treatment for suicidal thoughts and self-harm typically involves a multidisciplinary approach, including psychotherapy, medication, and ongoing support. Cognitive-behavioral therapy (CBT) is also often employed to address these thoughts and behaviors.

Prevention and Awareness: Awareness of the link between chronic anxiety and suicidal thoughts is crucial. Education about healthy coping strategies, the significance of emotional support, and the destigmatization of mental health are essential for prevention.

Support and Understanding: It is vital that those facing these challenges receive loving support and understanding from their loved ones. An environment of emotional support can make a significant difference in the recovery process.

Understanding the long-term effects of anxiety is vital for the implementation of prevention and early intervention strategies. Proper treatment and support are essential to mitigate these impacts and promote long-term mental health. A multidisciplinary approach involving mental health professionals is often necessary to provide a comprehensive and effective response to these challenges.

STRATEGIES TO MITIGATE THE IMPACTS OF ANXIETY ON MENTAL HEALTH

Effectively addressing anxiety is crucial to safeguard our long-term mental health and enhance our quality of life. There are several strategies that can assist in mitigating the detrimental impacts of anxiety:

Cognitive-Behavioral Therapy (CBT)

Cognitive-Behavioral Therapy (CBT) is a widely recognized and effective therapeutic approach in treating anxiety and various other mental disorders. It is based on the idea that our thoughts, emotions, and behaviors are interconnected and influence one another. In CBT, the therapist and the patient collaborate to identify and modify dysfunctional thought patterns that contribute to anxiety. Here is further information on how CBT operates in treating anxiety:

Identification of Dysfunctional Thoughts: A core principle of CBT is to help the patient identify automatic thoughts and distorted beliefs that fuel anxiety. These thoughts are often negative, irrational, and catastrophic, leading to a cycle of worry and fear.

Reassessment and Challenging of Thoughts: With guidance from the therapist, the patient learns to question the validity of these dysfunctional thoughts. They explore evidence for and against these thoughts and develop a more balanced and realistic perspective.

Development of Coping Skills: Besides challenging dysfunctional thoughts, CBT helps patients develop healthy coping skills. This may include relaxation strategies, problem-solving techniques, and gradual exposure practices to feared situations (a crucial component in treating phobias).

Identification of Behavior Patterns: CBT also focuses on identifying behavior patterns that may contribute to anxiety. For instance, avoiding feared situations can perpetuate anxiety. The therapist works with the patient to change these maladaptive behaviors.

Setting Goals and Monitoring Progress: During treatment, therapist and patient establish clear, measurable goals for anxiety reduction. Progress is monitored over time, allowing for adjustments as needed.

Between-Session Tasks: Patients often receive tasks to complete between sessions, such as maintaining a thought diary or practicing relaxation techniques. This helps integrate learning and skills into everyday life.

Duration and Effectiveness: CBT is a short-term therapy, usually consisting of a defined number of sessions (e.g., 12 to 16 sessions). It is known to be highly effective in treating anxiety disorders, providing practical tools and strategies to deal with anxiety in a healthy manner.

Adaptation to Different Anxiety Disorders: CBT can be tailored to treat a variety of anxiety disorders, including Generalized Anxiety Disorder (GAD), Panic Disorder, Post-Traumatic Stress Disorder (PTSD), specific phobias, and Obsessive-Compulsive Disorder (OCD).

CBT is often combined with other therapeutic approaches or medication, depending on the individual needs of the patient. It offers a solid framework for identifying, understanding, and overcoming anxiety, empowering individuals to regain control of their lives and enhance their mental health.

Meditation and Mindfulness

Meditation and mindfulness are ancient practices that have become increasingly popular in modern times due to their mental health benefits, including anxiety reduction. These practices focus on being fully aware of the present moment and paying mindful attention to thoughts, sensations, and emotions without judgment. Here is detailed information on how meditation and mindfulness can aid in reducing anxiety:

Mindfulness of the Present Moment: Meditation and mindfulness are based on the premise of being completely present in the current moment, free from concerns about the past or the future. This mindful awareness helps reduce anxiety, as anxiety is often linked to worries about the future.

Calming the Mind: Regular practice of meditation and mindfulness can calm the mind, reducing the constant stream of anxious thoughts. By focusing on the breath or other elements of the present moment, the mind becomes more tranquil.

Reducing Reactivity to Stress: By cultivating the ability to observe thoughts and emotions without impulsively reacting, mindfulness practices help reduce reactivity to stress. This can result in more thoughtful responses and fewer exaggerated emotional reactions.

Attention Training: Meditation and mindfulness are attention training exercises. They help develop the ability to focus attention on the present, which can be helpful in preventing the mind from wandering to worries and anxieties.

Reduction of Rumination: Rumination, or the continuous repetition of negative thoughts, is common in anxiety. Mindfulness can help interrupt this pattern by directing attention to the present, diverting it from negative thoughts and rumination.

Learning Acceptance and Tolerance: Mindfulness practices teach acceptance of thoughts and emotions without judgment, recognizing them as passing mental events. This fosters a more compassionate attitude towards oneself, which can reduce anxiety related to self-criticism.

Various Meditation Techniques: There are several meditation techniques, such as breath meditation, guided meditation, transcendental meditation, and walking meditation. Each of them can cater to different preferences and needs, allowing for adaptation of the practice according to the individual.

Regular and Consistent Practice: The key to reaping the benefits of meditation and mindfulness is regular and consistent practice. Allocating daily time for these practices can help integrate them into one's lifestyle and experience their positive effects over time.

Incorporating meditation and mindfulness into the daily routine can offer powerful tools to deal with anxiety and promote mental well-being. By learning to be more present in the moment, we can reduce anxiety associated with worrying about the future and thus live a more balanced and mindful life.

Physical Exercise

Regular practice of physical exercise is an effective and accessible strategy to alleviate anxiety and promote emotional well-being. The benefits extend beyond physical health, encompassing mental and emotional well-being. Let's delve into how physical exercises can contribute to anxiety reduction in detail:

Release of Endorphins: Physical exercises trigger the release of endorphins in the brain. Endorphins are neurotransmitters that act as natural analgesics and enhance mood, providing a sense of well-being and euphoria.

Reduction of Stress and Physical Tension: Regular exercise helps release accumulated physical tension, a common symptom associated with anxiety. As the body moves, muscles relax, and the sensation of physical stress diminishes.

Improved Blood Flow and Oxygenation: Exercises enhance blood flow and oxygenation throughout the body, including the brain. This can lead to improved mental clarity and a sense of freshness, alleviating the sense of oppression associated with anxiety.

Reduction of Stress Hormone Levels: Regular exercise can help reduce stress hormone levels, such as cortisol. These hormones are often elevated in individuals experiencing chronic anxiety.

Enhanced Sleep: Regular physical exercises can improve sleep quality, which is crucial for anxiety control.

Adequate sleep can regulate mood patterns and decrease the feeling of anxiety during the day.

Boost in Self-Esteem and Confidence: Engaging in physical activities can enhance self-image and boost self-confidence. Feeling good about one's body and achieving fitness goals can have a positive impact on self-perception.

Socialization Opportunities: Participating in group physical activities, such as sports or gym classes, provides opportunities for socialization. Social interaction can alleviate anxiety by providing a sense of belonging and social support.

Variety of Exercises: Exercise variety is important to maintain interest and motivation. This can include aerobic activities, resistance exercises, yoga, dance, among others. The choice of exercises should consider personal preferences and physical restrictions.

Adaptation to Personal Routine: It is crucial to choose an exercise type that fits into each individual's routine and lifestyle. This facilitates consistent incorporation of exercises into daily life.

Incorporating physical exercises into daily routine can be a highly effective way to manage and reduce anxiety, while offering a range of benefits for physical and mental health. It is important to find physical activities that are enjoyable and can be sustained in the long term to reap maximum benefits.

Controlled Breathing

The practice of controlled breathing techniques, such as diaphragmatic breathing, is an effective and accessible strategy to calm the nervous system and reduce anxiety. This approach focuses on breath awareness and control to promote a sense of calm and emotional balance. Let's explore in detail how controlled breathing can be a valuable tool in anxiety management:

Respiratory Awareness: The first step is to develop awareness of one's own breathing. Often, during moments of anxiety, breathing becomes shallow and rapid. Awareness allows recognizing this pattern and intervening to bring calmness.

Diaphragmatic Breathing: Also known as abdominal breathing, it is a technique that involves breathing deeply, expanding the diaphragm. During inhalation, the abdomen expands, and during exhalation, it contracts. This helps oxygenate the body more effectively and calm the mind.

Respiratory Rhythm: Establishing a rhythm in breathing is fundamental. A common technique is the 4-7-8 breathing, where you inhale through the nose counting to four, hold the breath in the lungs for seven seconds, and then exhale through the mouth counting to eight. This pattern promotes tranquility.

Focus on Breathing: During the practice of controlled breathing, it is important to maintain focus on the breath and the movements of the abdomen. This helps divert anxious thoughts, providing a moment of tranquility and concentration.

Reduction of Stress and Anxiety: Controlled breathing directly affects the nervous system, stimulating the relaxation response. This reduces stress and anxiety levels, promoting a sense of calm and mental clarity.

Regular Practice: To reap the benefits, regular practice is essential. Initially, practicing for a few minutes every day can be helpful, and over time, the duration and frequency of practice can be increased.

Integration with Other Techniques: Controlled breathing can be integrated with other relaxation techniques, such as meditation. This enhances the calming effects and promotes a deeper relaxation experience.

Application in Crisis Moments: The ability to use controlled breathing techniques in moments of acute anxiety or crisis is a valuable tool. It can be applied in stressful situations to calm the mind and prevent an escalation of anxiety.

Controlled breathing is a simple yet powerful tool that can be practiced anytime and anywhere. It is a valuable skill for managing anxiety, promoting well-being, and cultivating inner peace.

Acceptance and Commitment Therapy (ACT)

Acceptance and Commitment Therapy (ACT) is an effective therapeutic approach for dealing with anxiety, helping individuals accept their anxieties and difficulties, and commit to constructive and meaningful actions in their lives. Let's explore more about ACT and how it can be a valuable tool in anxiety management:

Acceptance of Internal Experiences: ACT emphasizes the importance of fully accepting our internal experiences, including emotions, thoughts, and physical sensations. This means not struggling or attempting to suppress these experiences, but rather acknowledging them and allowing them to be present.

Mindfulness and Mindful Awareness: The practice of mindfulness is central in ACT. It involves being aware of the present moment without judgment, which helps increase awareness of our internal experiences and respond to them in a more adaptive manner.

Defining Personal Values and Goals: ACT encourages the identification and definition of each individual's values and personal goals. Understanding what is truly important in life helps guide actions and make decisions aligned with these values.

Commitment to Action: In addition to acceptance, ACT encourages commitment to action. This means taking concrete steps in the direction of our values, even in the face of anxiety or discomfort. Action aligned with values is seen as a key component for a meaningful life.

Cognitive Defusion: This technique involves creating distance between ourselves and our thoughts and emotions. By "unsticking" from our thoughts and observing them as mental events, we are less likely to be dominated or defined by them, reducing the influence of anxiety.

Self-Awareness and Psychological Flexibility: ACT aims to increase self-awareness and psychological flexibility. This involves the ability to adapt and respond effectively to different situations, considering our values and goals.

Acceptance of Difficulties and Suffering: Instead of trying to avoid suffering, ACT invites us to accept the inevitable presence of human suffering. This does not mean resignation but rather courageous acceptance, allowing us to continue living our lives meaningfully.

Working with Metaphors and Experiences: ACT often utilizes metaphors and experiences to illustrate key concepts and facilitate understanding and application of the strategies. These stories help translate abstract concepts into something concrete and memorable.

ACT is a powerful approach for dealing with anxiety, as it provides a framework to accept challenging internal experiences while committing to meaningful actions. It helps cultivate a life based on values, resilience, and personal growth.

Establishing Wholesome Routines

Establishing wholesome routines stands as a crucial pillar for emotional equilibrium and well-being. A well-structured routine not only enhances efficiency in our daily activities but can also positively impact our mental and emotional health. Let us delve further into how establishing wholesome routines can reduce anxiety and promote a balanced lifestyle:

Regular Sleep Schedule: Establishing a consistent sleep schedule is paramount for adequate rest and maintaining emotional balance. Sufficient and regular sleep helps regulate mood, enhance concentration, and reduce anxiety.

Balanced Nutrition: Maintaining a well-rounded diet with a variety of nutritious foods is essential for mental health. Nutrient-rich foods can positively affect our mood and energy, providing a solid foundation to cope with stress and anxiety.

Time for Relaxing Activities: Integrating time for relaxing activities into the daily routine is crucial. This may include relaxation practices, reading, meditation, breathing exercises, or any hobby that brings tranquility. These moments help reduce stress and anxiety.

Structured Agenda: Creating a well-defined agenda for the day, week, or month can bring order and clarity. Knowing what to expect and having a plan helps reduce uncertainty, a trigger for anxiety.

Time for Physical Activity: Incorporating regular physical activity into the routine is a significant pillar. Exercise releases endorphins, chemicals that enhance mood, and helps alleviate stress and anxiety, promoting better mental health.

Adequate Breaks at Work: Establishing regular breaks during work is crucial for performance and well-being. Taking short breaks helps recharge energy and maintain focus, preventing stress accumulation throughout the day.

Time Management: Learning to manage time effectively is essential. This includes setting priorities, avoiding procrastination, and allocating time for essential tasks, which can reduce the feeling of being overwhelmed.

Flexibility in the Routine: While structure is important, it is also vital to include flexibility in the routine. Allowing for adjustments as needed to deal with unforeseen circumstances or simply to meet momentary needs.

Mental Hygiene: In addition to caring for the body, it is vital to dedicate time to mental health. This may include practices such as therapy, relaxation activities, reflection, or anything that nurtures mental health.

Establishing wholesome routines is not just about following a strict schedule but about creating an environment conducive to balance and well-being. It is a process that requires adaptability and self-awareness to find what works best for each individual, considering their needs and lifestyle. A healthy routine can become the anchor sustaining a balanced and less anxious life.

Relaxation Techniques

Relaxation techniques are potent tools for dealing with stress and anxiety. They allow us to slow down, calm the mind and body, and restore a state of tranquility. Let's explore some relaxation techniques that can be effective in reducing tension and promoting calm:

Progressive Muscle Relaxation: Progressive muscle relaxation, also known as progressive relaxation, is a technique where muscles are deliberately tensed and then relaxed. This helps release accumulated tension in the body, promoting a sense of relaxation.

Deep and Controlled Breathing: Practicing conscious, slow, and deep breathing can calm the nervous system. Inhaling slowly through the nose, holding the breath for a few seconds, and exhaling slowly through the mouth helps reduce anxiety and promote relaxation.

Guided Meditation: Guided meditation involves listening to an instructor leading a meditation session. Typically, this includes instructions on focusing on the breath, muscle relaxation, and visualization, helping to calm the mind and reduce anxiety.

Creative Visualization: In this technique, relaxing mental images are created to help calm the mind and body. Visualizing peaceful scenarios, like a sunny beach or a tranquil forest, can bring a sense of peace and relaxation.

Mindfulness and Mindful Awareness: Being fully present in the current moment, without judgment, is the essence of mindfulness. The practice of mindful awareness helps reduce anxiety by consciously focusing on sensations, thoughts, and emotions of the moment.

Biofeedback Techniques: These techniques involve using devices that monitor bodily functions such as heart rate and muscle tension. Real-time feedback allows the person to learn to control these functions, reducing the stress response.

Yoga and Stretching: Yoga combines physical exercises with breathing and meditation techniques, promoting physical and mental relaxation. Regular yoga practice can help relieve tension and anxiety.

Aromatherapy and Sensory Relaxation: Using essential oils and sensory techniques, such as massages or aromatic baths, can have a calming effect on the body and mind, promoting relaxation and stress reduction.

Chiropractic and Massage Techniques: Chiropractic and therapeutic massage can help release muscle tension and improve blood flow, contributing to an overall sense of relaxation and well-being.

Tai Chi or Qi Gong Practice: These practices combine gentle body movements, breathing, and mental focus. They are effective in reducing stress and enhancing emotional balance.

Relaxing Music and Nature Sounds: Listening to gentle music, nature sounds, or music specifically designed for relaxation can have a soothing effect on the mind, helping to alleviate anxiety.

The key to success with relaxation techniques is regular practice. Integrating them into the daily routine can make a significant difference in stress reduction and promoting an overall sense of calm and well-being. It's important to experiment with different techniques and discover those that best suit individual needs and preferences.

Creative Expression

Creative expression stands as a potent tool to grapple with anxiety and stress. It provides an outlet for our emotions, thoughts, and internal experiences, allowing them to be externalized and processed in a constructive manner. Let us delve into how art, music, and writing can be therapeutic and beneficial for mental health:

Art and Drawing: Art, be it painting, drawing, sculpture, or other forms, offers a way to express emotions that may be difficult to put into words. Colors, shapes, and textures can convey feelings and help alleviate anxiety by providing a creative channel to express what is within us.

Music and Melody: Music has the power to evoke emotions and create a profound connection with our own psyche. Playing an instrument, singing, or simply listening to music that resonates with us can alleviate stress and create a more tranquil state of mind.

Creative Writing: Writing is an effective way to process thoughts and emotions. Keeping a journal, writing poetry, stories, or simply putting on paper what we are feeling can help organize our thoughts and find emotional clarity.

Dance and Movement: Dance is a form of bodily expression that can release tension and anxiety. Moving to the rhythm of music allows energy to flow, promoting a sense of well-being.

Theatre and Performance: Engaging in theatrical or performance activities offers an opportunity to explore different roles and emotions, which can help better understand oneself and alleviate stress.

Craftsmanship and DIY (Do It Yourself): Engaging in craft projects, sewing, woodworking, or other DIY activities can be a tangible way to channel anxiety and create something beautiful at the same time.

Digital Art: Digital art provides a modern platform for creative expression. Digital painting, graphic design, and other forms of digital art enable a variety of means for artistic expression.

Bodily Expression: Bodily expression, including yoga, tai chi, and other physical practices, can help release emotions and create a sense of inner calm.

Art Therapy: Art therapy is a structured way of using creativity to explore emotions and psychological issues. It is often conducted by a trained therapist who guides the process.

Collaboration and Creative Groups: Participating in creative groups or collaborative projects can enhance the creative experience, providing the opportunity to share and learn from others.

Creative expression is a healthy and effective way to deal with anxiety, allowing you to process your emotions in a constructive and enriching manner. Each person is unique, so it's important to explore different forms of creative expression to find what resonates best with oneself.

Setting Boundaries and Saying No

Setting boundaries and learning to say no are vital aspects of self-care and effective stress management. Often, we feel social or personal pressure to meet the demands of others, which can lead to overcommitment and exhaustion. Let us delve deeper into this issue and understand how setting healthy boundaries can be transformative:

Protecting Your Well-being: Setting boundaries is a way to protect your physical and mental health. Saying no when necessary means acknowledging your own limits and not compromising your health and well-being.

Respecting Your Needs and Priorities: Each person has their own needs, priorities, and goals. Setting boundaries allows you to respect your priorities and dedicate time and energy to what truly matters to you.

Building Healthy Relationships: Clearly setting boundaries and communicating them respectfully helps build healthier relationships. People around you will understand your expectations and limits.

Learning to Say No Respectfully: Saying 'no' does not mean being rude, but rather being clear about your limitations and existing commitments. It can be a challenging skill, but it is fundamental to maintaining a healthy balance.

Avoiding Overload and Exhaustion: When you are always saying yes to everything and everyone, you can end up overwhelmed. This can lead to physical and mental exhaustion, impairing your productivity and well-being.

Setting Boundaries at Work: In the workplace, it is crucial to set boundaries for time, tasks, and availability. This helps maintain a balanced professional life and prevents burnout.

Practicing Clear and Direct Communication: Communication is key when setting boundaries. It's important to express your needs and expectations clearly and directly, without ambiguity.

Assessing Your Current Capacity: Before taking on new commitments, assess your current capacity to handle them. If you are overwhelmed, it's perfectly acceptable to say no or postpone.

Learning to Say Yes to Yourself: Saying no to others often means saying yes to yourself. It's an act of self-care and self-empowerment to recognize your needs and prioritize them.

Practicing Self-Control: Setting boundaries requires self-control and the ability to say "no" when necessary, even when there is external pressure.

Remembering that it is healthy and necessary to set boundaries is fundamental to maintaining a balanced and healthy life. It is an act of self-love and self-respect to learn to say no when necessary and protect your energy and well-being.

Seeking Social Support

Seeking social support is an essential strategy for dealing with anxiety and promoting emotional well-being. Social support can come from different sources, including friends, family, colleagues, and mental health professionals. Let us explore in detail how this connection with other individuals can be beneficial in alleviating anxiety:

Reducing Isolation: Sharing your concerns and feelings with others helps break the cycle of emotional isolation. Isolating oneself can escalate anxiety, and having a support system reduces this isolation.

Emotional Support: Talking to someone who understands your emotions and concerns can provide immense relief. Emotional support helps validate your feelings, reducing the sense of being alone in this struggle.

External Perspective: Friends and family can offer valuable perspectives and advice on the situation causing anxiety. Sometimes, an external view can illuminate solutions or options you hadn't considered.

Understanding and Empathy: The act of sharing can lead to a greater understanding of the challenges you are facing. Feeling understood and validated is essential for anxiety relief.

Stress Relief: Discussing your worries can be a way to relieve accumulated stress. Expressing emotions can reduce internal pressure that anxiety can create.

Building Healthy Connections: Seeking social support strengthens the bonds with people around you. Cultivating healthy relationships is fundamental for long-term mental and emotional health.

Seeking Professional Help: In addition to support from friends and family, seeking the help of a mental health professional, such as a psychologist or therapist, can provide expert guidance in dealing with anxiety more effectively.

Participating in Support Groups: Support groups are great options to meet people going through similar experiences. Sharing stories and strategies can be very comforting.

Practicing the Art of Listening: In addition to sharing your concerns, it's important to actively listen to others. Offering mutual support can strengthen relationships and create an effective support network.

Swift Intervention in Critical Moments: In crisis situations, social support can be crucial for intervening swiftly and providing appropriate help, potentially even saving lives.

Seeking social support is a valuable step in the journey to deal with anxiety. Strengthening social bonds, sharing concerns, and seeking advice from trustworthy individuals contribute to emotional resilience and reduce the impact of anxiety.

Practice of Self-Compassion

The practice of self-compassion is a fundamental approach to dealing with anxiety and enhancing mental health. Let us delve into the details of how this practice can be transformative and beneficial for your relationship with yourself:

Defining Self-Compassion: Self-compassion is the act of treating oneself with the same compassion, kindness, and understanding that one would offer to a dear friend in times of difficulty. It involves recognizing one's own humanity, imperfections, and challenges without harsh self-judgment.

Acceptance and Shared Humanity: Self-compassion begins with self-acceptance, acknowledging that you are human and, as such, subject to flaws, errors, and challenges. It is about understanding that everyone, without exception, faces difficulties, and this is part of the human experience.

Self-Empathy and Self-Understanding: Cultivating self-compassion involves developing an inner voice that speaks to you in a kind and encouraging manner, rather than harsh self-criticism. It's about treating yourself as you would someone you love and deeply care for.

Emotional Resilience: Regular practice of self-compassion strengthens your emotional resilience. Instead of letting self-criticism drain your energies, you learn to rise after challenges, learning and growing from them.

Reducing Anxiety: By adopting a compassionate attitude toward oneself, you reduce the anxiety associated with the fear of not being good enough or making mistakes. Self-compassion calms the mind and lessens internal pressure.

Combating Shame: Self-compassion is a powerful tool to combat shame and self-criticism. Instead of being ashamed of your imperfections, you embrace yourself with love and understanding.

Cultivating Gratitude and Acceptance: The practice of self-compassion is linked to gratitude for who you are, with all your characteristics and experiences. This leads to a deep acceptance of oneself, which, in turn, contributes to a calmer mind.

Self-Compassion Techniques: Self-compassion can be practiced through various techniques, such as loving-kindness meditation, where you wish love and happiness for yourself and others; writing kind letters to yourself; or simply changing the internal narrative to one of care and compassion.

Integration into Daily Life: Besides specific practices, self-compassion can be a philosophy of life. This means bringing kindness into all areas of your life, whether at work, in relationships, or in your daily activities.

Self-Care: Self-compassion is also reflected in self-care. You treat yourself well, establish healthy boundaries, and allow yourself to rest and rejuvenate.

Self-compassion is a powerful skill that can be cultivated and developed. By practicing kindness and compassion towards yourself, you strengthen your emotional resilience, reduce anxiety, and create a healthier foundation for dealing with life's challenges.

Stress Assessment and Coping Strategies

Assessing stress and developing effective coping strategies are valuable skills for managing anxiety and promoting emotional well-being. Let us explore in detail how you can identify and confront stress adaptively:

Identifying Sources of Stress: The first step is to recognize and identify the sources of stress in your life. This may include work challenges, relationship issues, financial concerns, among others. Being aware of these sources is crucial for effectively dealing with stress.

Assessing the Impact of Stress: Understand how stress affects you physically, emotionally, and mentally. Stress can manifest in various ways, such as insomnia, irritability, anxiety, headaches, among others. Evaluate how stress is impacting your quality of life.

Consequences of Not Managing Stress: Recognize the consequences of not effectively dealing with stress. This may include worsening physical health, deterioration of personal relationships, poor performance at work or in studies, among others.

Self-awareness and Self-Care: Get to know yourself, your limitations, and your needs. Regularly practice self-care by dedicating time to activities that rejuvenate and bring you joy. This can include exercise, hobbies, meditation, among others.

Developing Coping Strategies: Learn and develop effective coping strategies. This may include relaxation techniques, exercise, meditation, therapy, or talking to a friend or mental health professional. Each person may respond differently, so it's important to experiment and find what works best for you.

Planning and Organization: Plan your activities and commitments. Organization can reduce stress associated with feeling overwhelmed. Set realistic goals and create a plan to achieve them.

Seeking Professional Help: Do not hesitate to seek help from a mental health professional, such as a psychologist or therapist. They can provide specialized guidance and personalized strategies for dealing with stress.

Regular Relaxation Practice: Adopt regular relaxation practices, such as breathing techniques, yoga, or progressive muscle relaxation. These practices can help alleviate the physical and mental tension associated with stress.

Continuous Assessment and Adjustments: Regularly evaluate the effectiveness of your coping strategies. If something is not working, adjust your approaches and try new strategies to find what best suits you.

Conscious assessment of stress and implementing effective coping strategies are essential steps in dealing with anxiety adaptively. Developing emotional resilience and knowing how to confront life's challenges can significantly improve your quality of life and well-being.

Consulting Mental Health Professionals

When grappling with severe or persistent anxiety, it is pivotal to seek the guidance of mental health professionals for specialized insight and appropriate treatment. Below, you will find details regarding the significance and the process of seeking professional support to address anxiety:

The Importance of Seeking Professional Help: Anxiety can manifest in various forms and intensities, and in some instances, managing it alone can prove challenging.

Mental health professionals possess the requisite training and experience to assess, diagnose, and effectively treat anxiety disorders.

Types of Mental Health Professionals: There exist several types of mental health professionals who can assist in anxiety treatment, including psychologists, psychiatrists, occupational therapists, clinical social workers, among others. Each employs a specific approach and may be recommended depending on the situation and individual needs.

The Role of Psychologists: Psychologists are experts in evaluating and treating mental health issues, including anxiety. They employ therapeutic techniques, such as cognitive-behavioral therapy, to assist individuals in understanding and modifying dysfunctional thought patterns that contribute to anxiety.

The Role of Psychiatrists: Psychiatrists are medical specialists in diagnosing, treating, and preventing mental disorders, including anxiety. They can prescribe medications, if necessary, and may integrate pharmacological treatments with therapy for a comprehensive approach.

Procedure for Seeking Assistance: Begin by researching and identifying mental health professionals in your vicinity. You can seek recommendations from physicians, friends, or family. Ensure that the professional is licensed and has experience in anxiety treatment.

Scheduling an Appointment: Reach out to the chosen professional to schedule a consultation. During the initial consultation, you will discuss your symptoms, medical history, and any concerns you may have. This initial consultation allows the professional to comprehend your situation and propose a treatment plan.

Assessment and Diagnosis: During the consultation, the mental health professional will conduct a thorough assessment to diagnose the type and severity of anxiety. The diagnosis is pivotal for devising an effective treatment plan.

Personalized Treatment Plan: Following the assessment, the mental health professional will create a personalized treatment plan that may encompass therapy, medication, coping strategies, and lifestyle changes.

Follow-up and Adjustments: It is imperative to adhere to the proposed treatment plan and attend follow-up consultations. If necessary, the plan can be adjusted based on progress or changing needs.

Active Participation in Treatment: Active participation in treatment is essential. Share information about your progress, concerns, and perceived changes, enabling the professional to adapt the treatment as needed.

Seeking help from mental health professionals is a critical step in managing anxiety. They will provide guidance, support, and the necessary tools to help you overcome the challenges related to anxiety and enhance your quality of life.

These strategies can be combined and tailored according to individual preferences and needs, offering a comprehensive approach to mitigate the impacts of anxiety on mental health. It is important to remember that each person responds differently, so finding what works best for each individual is fundamental.

Anxiety is a potent force capable of shaping our internal world in profound and intricate ways. In this chapter, we explore the ramifications of this emotional storm in the realm of mental health. From anxiety disorders to the loss of self-esteem, each impact is a stone that shifts the foundation of our mental health. Understanding the breadth of this impact is crucial for our journey toward healing and balance.

We must not forget that anxiety also manifests in the physical body, with somatic symptoms that can at times be confused with medical conditions. In the next chapter, we will venture into an equally vital yet often underestimated territory: the physical effects of anxiety. Just as the mind and emotion, our body is an active participant in this dance. Anxiety intertwines with our biology, influencing our physical well-being in surprising ways. Let us delve into this complex ocean of connections between mind and body, exploring how our physical health is impacted by anxiety and how we can find tranquility amidst this tempest.

6

IMPACTS ON PHYSICAL HEALTH

The body speaks the language of anxiety; listen and tend, for we are works of art in constant restoration.

Anxiety, this emotional and physiological reaction that we all experience at some point in our lives, is a powerful and multifaceted force. It is a response from our organism to stress, an ancient mechanism that readies us to confront perceived threats, mobilizing our energies and focus to overcome challenges. However, when this response becomes chronic, uncontrolled, and disproportionate to real situations, it ceases to be our ally and transforms into a constant source of distress and disturbance.

In this chapter, we delve into the realm of the effects anxiety can have on our physical health. It is not merely a burden on our minds; it is a load our bodies carry as well. Anxiety goes beyond triggering a fight-or-flight response; it influences our nervous system, our musculature, our sleep patterns, and ultimately, our overall physical health.

We will explore the effects of this prolonged anxiety, such as the manifestation of physical pains, persistent muscle tension, and sleep disorders. We will understand how this stress response affects our organs, our immune system, and our overall physical well-being. Furthermore, we will discuss strategies and approaches to mitigate these harmful impacts on physical health, intending to provide paths to alleviate the burden that anxiety places on our body.

As we prepare for this plunge into the physical impact of anxiety, it is imperative to remember that our body and mind are intricately interconnected. What affects one impacts the other. Thus, in addressing the effects of anxiety on physical health, we are also, indirectly, speaking about its effect on mental health and vice versa. It is a complex and vital dance that we must comprehend to enhance our quality of life and promote a comprehensive and balanced health.

EFFECTS OF ANXIETY ON OUR BODY

When we find ourselves in a state of anxiety, our body reacts as if we were in peril, activating a stress response known as 'fight or flight.' This response triggers a series of physiological reactions that manifest in various and often distressing ways:

Physical Aches

Anxiety can have notable physical manifestations, and one of the most common forms is through aches in different parts of the body. These aches can vary in intensity and location and are often triggered by muscle tension resulting from anxiety. Let us delve into more details about this phenomenon:

Common Locations of Physical Aches: Anxiety can manifest as physical aches in various parts of the body, including the head, neck, shoulders, back, and stomach. The most affected areas tend to be those where muscle tension accumulates due to constant stress and anxiety.

Muscle Tension and Aches: Muscle tension, a physical response to stress and anxiety, is a defense mechanism of the body. However, chronic tension can lead to headaches, migraines, backaches, and abdominal discomfort, among other symptoms.

Pain-Anxiety Cycle: A harmful cycle can develop when physical aches caused by anxiety lead to more anxiety, creating a loop where pain generates more anxiety and vice versa. Breaking this cycle can be challenging without appropriate interventions.

Mind-Body Connection: The body and mind are deeply interconnected. Emotional stress and anxiety can manifest physically due to the release of stress hormones and muscle tension. Similarly, physical discomfort can affect our mental health and emotional well-being.

Nervous System Response: Anxiety activates the sympathetic nervous system, triggering fight-or-flight physical reactions. This can result in increased heart rate, rapid breathing, and muscle tension, contributing to the sensation of pain and discomfort.

Relief Strategies: To interrupt the pain-anxiety cycle, it is essential to adopt strategies that aim to alleviate both physical pain and anxiety. This can include physical therapies like therapeutic massage and relaxation techniques such as meditation and deep breathing.

Healthcare Professional: If physical aches persist or worsen, it is important to seek guidance from a healthcare professional. They can help assess and offer specific treatments to alleviate the pain and address the underlying anxiety.

Physical aches can become chronic if anxiety persists, leading to a cycle where pain generates more anxiety and vice versa. Understanding the relationship between anxiety and physical aches is crucial to adopt effective management approaches that consider both the emotional and physical aspects of well-being. Integrated treatment, which considers the interaction between body and mind, is often the most effective in dealing with these complex interconnections.

Sleep Disorders

The relationship between anxiety and sleep disorders is complex and can create a vicious cycle that significantly affects sleep quality and anxiety. Let us delve deeper into this subject:

Common Sleep Disorders Associated with Anxiety: Anxiety can cause various sleep disorders, including insomnia, difficulty falling asleep, staying asleep, and frequent nightmares. These disorders result from the inability to calm the mind before sleep due to persistent anxiety.

Negative Cycle between Anxiety and Sleep: Anxiety can trigger sleep disorders, and the lack of adequate sleep can worsen anxiety. This forms a negative cycle where anxiety disrupts sleep, and sleep deprivation increases anxiety, creating a harmful loop.

Restless Mind and Nighttime Restlessness: The restless and worried mind, common in anxious individuals, can prevent the body and mind from calming down enough for restorative sleep. Ceaseless thoughts and worries can keep a person awake or interrupt sleep during the night.

Impact of Sleep Deprivation on Anxiety: Lack of adequate sleep negatively affects our ability to cope with stress and regulate our emotions. This amplifies anxiety symptoms, making it harder to deal with day-to-day situations.

Restorative Sleep and Mental Health: Restorative sleep is vital for mental health. During sleep, the brain processes emotions and events of the day, consolidates memories, and recharges the mind for the next day. Sleep deprivation can impair these fundamental functions.

Strategies to Improve Sleep: Adopting a consistent sleep routine, creating a sleep-friendly environment, avoiding caffeine and electronics before bedtime, and practicing relaxation techniques can help improve sleep quality and, consequently, reduce associated anxiety.

Professional Intervention: If sleep disorders persist and significantly affect the quality of life, it is crucial to seek help from a mental health professional. They can assess and offer specific treatments to improve sleep and address the underlying anxiety.

Understanding the physical effects of anxiety is a crucial part of what makes this condition so debilitating. Understanding how anxiety affects the body is fundamental to seek effective management strategies that target not only the mind but also physical health, promoting a comprehensive balance for our well-being.

LONG-TERM EFFECTS OF ANXIETY ON OUR PHYSICAL HEALTH

Anxiety, when chronic and inadequately managed, can have enduring and substantial impacts on our physical health. These long-term effects manifest in diverse ways, affecting different systems and organs of our body:

Cardiovascular System

Chronic anxiety can exert additional pressure on the cardiovascular system, increasing the risk of heart diseases. Continuous exposure to high levels of stress hormones, such as cortisol and adrenaline, can lead to elevated heart rate, high blood pressure, and other cardiovascular risk factors. Over time, this can contribute to the development of cardiac conditions such as hypertension, arrhythmias, and coronary artery disease.

Immune System

Chronic anxiety can compromise the immune system, making us more susceptible to infections and illnesses. Prolonged stress can suppress immune function, reducing the effectiveness of our natural defenses against pathogens. This can result in a higher number of infections, colds, and other ailments, affecting our quality of life and well-being.

Respiratory System

Anxiety can affect the respiratory system, leading to symptoms such as rapid breathing, shortness of breath, and a sensation of suffocation. In the long run, this inadequate breathing can contribute to the development of chronic respiratory problems, such as hyperventilation syndrome. Anxiety can also exacerbate preexisting respiratory conditions like asthma and chronic obstructive pulmonary disease (COPD).

Digestive System

Chronic anxiety can wreak havoc on the digestive system, causing issues like irritable bowel syndrome (IBS), ulcers, acid reflux, and other gastrointestinal disorders. Prolonged stress can affect gastrointestinal tract motility, causing abdominal discomfort, diarrhea, constipation, and pain.

Musculoskeletal System

Chronic muscle tension resulting from anxiety can lead to long-term musculoskeletal problems. Persistent tension can cause muscular aches, stiffness, and joint wear and tear, affecting mobility and quality of life.

Central Nervous System

Chronic anxiety can alter the structure and function of the brain over time. Studies indicate that areas of the brain involved in emotion processing and stress response may be adversely affected by persistent anxiety. These alterations may be related to an increased risk of neurological and psychiatric disorders.

Understanding these long-term effects of anxiety on physical health is crucial in recognizing the importance of addressing anxiety in a holistic manner. Effective anxiety management strategies aim not only to alleviate immediate symptoms but also to safeguard and promote long-term physical health.

STRATEGIES TO MITIGATE THE PHYSICAL IMPACTS OF ANXIETY

Anxiety can exert significant pressure on our bodies, resulting in various adverse physical effects. However, there are effective strategies that can be implemented to help alleviate and mitigate these negative impacts on our physical well-being. These are effective approaches to mitigating the physical impacts of anxiety:

Physical Exercise Practice

Regular exercise is a powerful tool for alleviating the physical effects of anxiety. It helps release endorphins, the neurotransmitters of well-being, reducing muscle tension, improving sleep, and relieving stress. Any form of physical activity, whether it's walking, running, yoga, or swimming, can be beneficial.

Relaxation Techniques

Incorporating relaxation techniques into daily routines, such as meditation, deep breathing, progressive muscle relaxation, and biofeedback, can reduce muscle tension and calm the nervous system. These techniques help decrease the stress response, promoting a sense of calm and tranquility.

Healthy Eating

A balanced and healthy diet can have a positive impact on anxiety and its associated physical effects. Avoiding excess caffeine, sugar, and processed foods can help stabilize mood and energy, reducing the tendency for sharp fluctuations. Opting for nutrient-rich foods and vitamins, such as fruits, vegetables, whole grains, and lean proteins, can support physical and emotional health.

Adequate Sleep

Ensuring an adequate amount of quality sleep is essential to combat the effects of anxiety on sleep. Regular sleep hygiene practices, such as maintaining a consistent sleep schedule, creating a conducive sleeping environment, and limiting exposure to electronic devices before bedtime, can improve sleep quality and, in turn, reduce physical symptoms related to anxiety.

Leisure and Recreational Activities

Engaging in leisure and recreational activities that bring pleasure and relaxation, such as hobbies, reading, art, music, or spending time outdoors, can help reduce anxiety and its physical effects. These activities promote a break from everyday stress, allowing moments of relaxation and rejuvenation.

Occupational Therapy

Occupational therapy or physiotherapy can be beneficial in alleviating the physical effects of anxiety, especially muscle tension. Professionals can teach specific stretching and relaxation exercises, as well as techniques to improve posture and mobility, reducing pain and discomfort.

Psychological Therapy

Cognitive-Behavioral Therapy (CBT) and other therapeutic approaches can help manage anxiety, reducing its physical impacts. These therapies aid in identifying negative thought patterns and developing skills to cope with stress more effectively.

Medical Supervision

In severe cases of anxiety with significant physical effects, supervision by a healthcare professional, such as a doctor or psychiatrist, is essential. They can recommend medications or other appropriate interventions to alleviate physical and emotional symptoms.

In this chapter, we have thoroughly explored the effects that anxiety exerts on our physical bodies. Anxiety is not merely a mental phenomenon but something that manifests in our bodies in complex and often debilitating ways. From physical pains to sleep disorders, we have seen how anxiety can profoundly impact our physical health. Understanding these effects is crucial to develop strategies that help us mitigate the impact of anxiety on our physical well-being.

Embracing strategies to mitigate the physical impacts of anxiety as part of a comprehensive approach to managing it can have a positive impact on our physical and emotional health. Keep in mind that each person is unique, so it's important to experiment with and adapt these strategies according to your needs and preferences. The key is to seek a balance that promotes a healthier and happier life.

In the next chapter, we will understand that anxiety is often a vicious cycle, where symptoms feed off each other, creating a downward spiral. By understanding this dynamic, we can begin to break this cycle and find ways to interrupt its negative progression.

7
THE VICIOUS CYCLE OF ANXIETY

Break the chains of the vicious cycle, discover your liberation, and breathe the air of tranquility.

Anxiety is a powerful force that can embed itself in our lives, creating a vicious cycle that seems insurmountable. It is a complex experience, often initiated by triggering situations that evoke intense emotional responses. However, what unfolds thereafter is a complex interplay of physiological, behavioral, and emotional responses, forming a downward spiral that affects every aspect of our being.

In this chapter, we delve into the heart of this vicious cycle. We shall unveil its layers, understand its gears, and most importantly, learn to break it. By comprehending the self-perpetuating cycle of anxiety, we can adopt specific and intentional strategies to interrupt it and promote full recovery.

UNDERSTANDING THE SELF-PERPETUATING CYCLE OF ANXIETY

Anxiety is not an isolated event; it is a complex and interactive process that can morph into a self-perpetuating cycle. A deep understanding of this cycle is crucial to unravel how anxiety persists and even intensifies over time. Let us thoroughly explore the mechanisms involved in the vicious cycle of anxiety.

Initial Triggers: The Onset of the Cycle

The anxiety cycle begins with the initial triggers, which are situations, events, or stimuli that initiate the chain of reactions culminating in the experience of anxiety. Let us delve more deeply into this crucial stage of the anxiety cycle:

Nature of Triggers: Triggers can be diverse, including workplace stressors, past traumatic events, uncertainties about the future, specific phobias (such as fear of flying, spiders, confined spaces), or even a reaction to a particular environment, such as large crowds or open spaces.

Individuality of Triggers: Each person has their unique sensitivities and distinct triggers that set off anxiety. What might trigger one person may not affect another in the same manner. This individuality results from life experiences, personality, personal history, and other factors shaping each individual's perceptions and responses.

Variety of Triggers: Triggers can vary in intensity and frequency. Some triggers may be occasional, while others may be persistent. They may arise unexpectedly or be predictable. The wide range of triggers necessitates personalized understanding in the process of managing anxiety.

Reactions to Triggers: Reactions to triggers may encompass an immediate emotional response, such as fear, anxiety, panic, sadness, or anger. These emotional reactions often trigger a cascade of physical, cognitive, and behavioral responses, setting off the anxiety cycle.

Connection to Past Experiences: Past traumas, negative experiences, or even positive ones can shape sensitivity to triggers. Associating a current situation with past experiences can intensify the anxiety reaction, creating a link between the past and the present.

Identification and Management: Identifying triggers is a fundamental step in managing anxiety. This enables the development of appropriate coping strategies to deal with these situations in a healthy and constructive manner, thereby breaking the vicious cycle of anxiety.

Understanding the nature and individuality of initial triggers is crucial to develop effective coping strategies and break the cycle of anxiety. By recognizing and comprehending what triggers anxiety, individuals can work on prevention and effective management of these situations to enhance their quality of life and emotional well-being.

Fight or Flight Response: Activation of the Body

The fight or flight response is an automatic and instinctive reaction that occurs in the face of perceived threats. In anxiety, this response is triggered by the autonomic nervous system, resulting in a series of physical and hormonal changes. Let's delve deeper into understanding this fundamental response in the anxiety cycle:

Nature of the Fight or Flight Response: The fight or flight response is a primitive response designed to prepare the organism to face or flee from a perceived threat. Even in modern situations, this response persists and can be triggered by stimuli perceived as dangerous or stressful.

Autonomic Nervous System: The autonomic nervous system, consisting of the sympathetic and parasympathetic nervous systems, plays a central role in the fight or flight response. When activated, it readies the body for immediate action.

Release of Stress Hormones: Activation of the fight or flight response triggers the release of stress hormones, such as adrenaline and cortisol, into the bloodstream. These hormones prepare the body for an effective response to the perceived threat.

Adrenaline: Adrenaline is a hormone that readies the body for immediate action. It increases heart rate, raises blood pressure, dilates airways, boosts available energy, and sharpens the senses. These physical changes prepare the body to react swiftly.

Cortisol: Cortisol is another hormone released during the fight or flight response. It raises blood glucose to provide quick energy to muscles and the brain. Cortisol also suppresses non-essential functions during stress, such as digestion.

Preparatory Physical Reactions: In addition to hormone release, the body responds with immediate physical changes, including pupil dilation, increased heart rate, rapid and shallow breathing, increased sweating, and muscle contraction. These reactions prepare the body for action, whether to fight the threat or flee from it.

Evolutionary Purpose: The fight or flight response played a crucial role in the survival of our human ancestors, allowing for rapid reactions to predators or dangerous situations. Although our modern life presents different challenges, this response continues to be activated in stressful and anxiety-inducing situations.

Understanding the body's activation during the fight or flight response in anxiety is crucial to address the anxiety cycle effectively. Stress and anxiety management strategies can be targeted to modulate this response and promote a balance between stress reaction and emotional well-being.

Physical and Emotional Manifestations: Anxiety Sensations

When the fight or flight response is triggered by anxiety, it manifests in various physical and emotional sensations that can be overwhelming and intensify the feeling of anxiety. Let's delve deeper into these manifestations:

Increased Heart Rate: One of the common physical manifestations is an accelerated heart rate. The heart begins to beat faster as part of the preparation for a possible confrontation.

Shallow or Rapid Breathing: Breathing may become shallower and quicker. This occurs to ensure that the body receives enough oxygen to face the perceived threatening situation.

Muscle Tension: Activation of the autonomic nervous system during anxiety results in widespread muscle tension. Muscles may become contracted and rigid, contributing to uncomfortable sensations.

Excessive Sweating: Anxiety can trigger excessive sweating, resulting in sweaty palms, sweaty hands, and in some cases, generalized sweating.

Dizziness and Vertigo: Some individuals may experience dizziness or a sense of vertigo. This is related to the response of the inner ear's vestibular system to stress.

Gastrointestinal Discomfort: Anxiety can affect the gastrointestinal tract, leading to sensations of abdominal discomfort, nausea, or diarrhea.

Restlessness and Agitation: Anxious individuals often exhibit physical restlessness, such as leg fidgeting, foot tapping, or constant fidgeting with hands.

Intrusive Thoughts: The mind can be inundated with worrisome and intrusive thoughts related to the stressful situation. These thoughts can become obsessive.

Intensified Fear and Worries: The fight or flight response can amplify fear and worry about the triggering situation, resulting in a spiral of anxiety.

Sense of Imminent Danger: A general sense of imminent danger or an impending threat is common during an episode of anxiety activated by the fight or flight cycle.

These physical and emotional manifestations of anxiety can be overwhelming and contribute to a persistent cycle of anxiety. Understanding these manifestations is crucial to develop effective coping strategies, including relaxation techniques, meditation, and cognitive-behavioral therapy, aimed at calming the body and mind, breaking the anxiety cycle, and promoting mental recovery.

Negative Thought Patterns: Cognitive Cycle

Negative thought patterns play a fundamental role in the anxiety cycle, influencing how we perceive and respond to triggering situations. Let's delve more deeply into this cognitive cycle and how it relates to anxiety:

Worst-Case Anticipation: During an anxiety episode, the mind tends to anticipate the worst possible scenario regarding the triggering situation. This excessive and pessimistic anticipation can intensify anxiety.

Catastrophizing: The tendency to catastrophize is amplified in anxiety. People may envision the worst outcomes of a situation, even if they are highly unlikely. This amplification of danger can lead to an exponential increase in anxiety.

Excessive Worry: The anxious mind can enter a cycle of excessive worry. Thoughts continue to revolve around the situation, often repeating the same fears and uncertainties, leading to an escalation of anxiety levels.

Self-Deprecating Thoughts: During anxiety, self-esteem can be compromised. Individuals may have negative thoughts about themselves, doubting their abilities and competencies. These self-deprecating thoughts can intensify anxiety.

Constant Self-Criticism: Self-criticism is common in anxiety. People may criticize themselves relentlessly, focusing on perceived mistakes or supposed flaws, which can further fuel anxiety and fear.

Rumination about the Past: The anxious mind often gets stuck in past events, revisiting situations where they felt anxious or insecure. This habit of rumination can intensify anxiety by reinforcing negative thought patterns.

Exaggeration of Situation Severity: Negative thought patterns can lead to an exaggerated view of the severity of the situation. Concerns can be magnified, resulting in excessive anxiety.

Hypervigilance: Anxiety can lead to excessive vigilance regarding potential threats. This means individuals are constantly alert to signs of danger, perpetuating the anxiety cycle.

Understanding these thought patterns is essential to address anxiety effectively. Changing cognitive patterns can disrupt the negative cycle and promote better mental health.

Avoidance and Safety Behaviors: Adaptive Responses

Avoidance and safety behaviors are strategies that individuals employ to cope with anxiety. Let us delve deeper into our understanding of these adaptive responses and how they influence the anxiety cycle:

Avoidance: Avoidance involves steering clear or distancing oneself from situations, activities, or places perceived as anxiety-inducing triggers. This may encompass evading social gatherings, crowded spaces, public presentations, or any scenario that elicits discomfort. Avoidance provides immediate relief but sustains anxiety in the long term as the individual does not confront and overcome their worries.

Seeking Reassurance: Some individuals seek reassurances to feel more secure in anxious situations. This may involve repeatedly seeking others' opinions to validate their decisions, constantly seeking information about a situation, or performing repetitive checks to ensure everything is in order. This quest for reassurances temporarily alleviates anxiety but does not address the underlying cause.

Repetitive Rituals: Repetitive rituals, also known as compulsions, are actions or behaviors performed repetitively in response to anxiety. These can include excessive handwashing, repeatedly checking doors, compulsive counting, or specific movements. These rituals provide a sense of temporary control over anxiety but in the long run, contribute to its maintenance.

Avoidance of Uncomfortable Situations: Avoiding anxiety-triggering situations is a common form of avoidance behavior. People may avoid social situations, work challenges, or even daily activities they fear might trigger anxiety. Avoidance limits exposure to anxiety but also restricts personal growth and overcoming concerns.

Dependency on "Comfort Zones": Some individuals create comfort zones where they feel safe and less anxious. They may cling to specific environments or activities that provide them comfort, refusing to venture out of these zones. While they may experience temporary relief, this dependency on comfort zones does not address the underlying anxiety and may lead to a constrained life.

Patterns of Generalized Avoidance: Over time, avoidance can become generalized, leading to avoiding a wide range of situations. This restricts the person's life, creating barriers to personal growth and goal achievement.

These avoidance and safety behaviors are understood as coping mechanisms that offer momentary relief from anxiety. However, in the long run, they sustain anxiety and contribute to the persistence of the anxiety cycle.

Cycle Reinforcement: Learning and Conditioning

Deepening our understanding of how anxiety perpetuates, let's explore the reinforcement phase of the cycle, involving learning and conditioning. This process plays a crucial role in the persistence and intensification of anxiety over time:

Associative Learning: Each time a person experiences the fight or flight response in a specific anxious situation, an associative learning process occurs in the brain. It associates the stimuli or triggering situations with the feelings of anxiety they experienced. For example, if a person feels anxiety during a public presentation, their mind associates that specific situation (stage, audience, etc.) with anxiety symptoms.

Reinforcement of Anxiety: This associative learning reinforces the anxiety response. Each time the person is exposed to the feared situation, the brain reaffirms this anxious association. Thus, anxiety increases and becomes an automatic response to these stimuli.

Classical Conditioning: This process is akin to classical conditioning, a widely studied concept in psychology. The original neutral stimulus (the situation) becomes a conditioned stimulus that elicits an anxious response similar to the actual situation. The brain learns to anticipate anxiety in the presence of these conditioned stimuli.

Sensitization: Over time and repetition of this process, sensitization occurs. This means that anxiety intensifies over time, becoming more pronounced and difficult to control. The anxiety cycle perpetuates, and facing feared situations can become even more challenging.

Difficulty in Breaking the Cycle: Sensitization and conditioning result in a self-perpetuating cycle. The brain is now highly sensitized to associate these stimuli with anxiety, making interrupting the cycle more challenging. Even initially non-anxious situations may start to evoke anxiety due to this conditioning.

Understanding this reinforcement dynamics is crucial to effectively address anxiety.

Perseverance and Intensification: The Perpetual Cycle

Let us delve deeper into our understanding of the phase of perseverance and intensification in the self-perpetuating cycle of anxiety, comprehending how this cycle strengthens and endures over time:

Automatization of the Anxious Response: As the anxiety cycle repeats, the anxious response becomes automated. The brain creates a strong and swift connection between the triggers and the anxiety response, leading to an almost instantaneous reaction.

Broadening the Spectrum of Anxious Situations: Over time, anxiety can generalize beyond the initial situations or stimuli. Initially associated with certain triggers, anxiety begins to be triggered by a broader range of related or unrelated stimuli.

Mutually Reinforcing Cycle: The intensification of anxiety and its generalization result in a cycle that mutually reinforces itself. Generalized anxiety amplifies the perception of perceived danger, fueling the cycle and making it harder to interrupt.

Difficulty Distinguishing Cause and Effect: With the intensification of the cycle, it becomes challenging for the individual to discern what came first: the anxiety or the situation that triggers it. This process complicates the precise identification of the roots of anxiety, hindering effective intervention.

Unconscious Perpetuation: Part of this cycle occurs unconsciously. Anxious response patterns can be so automatic and subtle that the individual may not consciously realize they are caught in this self-perpetuating cycle.

Need for Conscious Intervention: Given the automatization and generalization of anxiety, conscious effort and therapeutic intervention are necessary to break this cycle. Specific therapeutic strategies such as exposure techniques, cognitive restructuring, and emotional regulation are vital to help interrupt the intensification and persistence of anxiety.

Understanding this phase of the self-perpetuating cycle is crucial for devising effective therapeutic strategies that can challenge and modify these patterns, promoting a more adaptive response to anxiety-triggering situations and thus breaking the persistent cycle of anxiety.

By identifying intervention points and implementing effective strategies, we can halt the self-perpetuating cycle and embark on our journey towards recovery and mental well-being.

METHODS TO BREAK THE CYCLE AND FOSTER RECOVERY

Breaking the self-perpetuating cycle of anxiety is essential to alleviate distress and promote improved mental and physical health. Let us explore effective strategies and methods to interrupt this vicious cycle and initiate the recovery process.

Awareness and Education

The first crucial step is awareness of the nature of the anxiety cycle. Understanding how triggers, physical responses, and thought patterns are interconnected is fundamental. Education about anxiety, its symptoms, and its effects helps individuals recognize when the cycle is starting and take measures to interrupt it.

Practice of Gradual Exposure

Gradual exposure is one of the most effective strategies for overcoming avoidance. Begin gradually exposing yourself to situations that trigger anxiety, starting with the least feared ones. Slowly face more challenging situations. This helps deactivate the anxiety response and show your brain that the situation is not as perilous as it seems.

Relaxation Techniques

Relaxation practices such as deep breathing, meditation, yoga, and mindfulness can help reduce activation of the sympathetic nervous system. By calming the body and mind, you can interrupt the anxiety cycle by reducing the physical stress response.

Seeking Professional Help

A mental health professional, such as a psychologist or psychiatrist, can provide specialized guidance in understanding and dealing with anxiety. Cognitive-behavioral therapy (CBT) is a common and highly effective treatment for anxiety disorders.

Healthy Lifestyle

Maintaining a healthy lifestyle, including a balanced diet, regular exercise, and adequate sleep, can help balance neurotransmitters and promote a more stable mental state, assisting in breaking the cycle of anxiety.

Learning Coping Strategies

Developing healthy coping skills, such as problem-solving, positive thinking, and assertive communication, can help deal with triggering situations more effectively, thus breaking the cycle of anxiety.

Mindfulness Practice

Regular mindfulness practice helps stay in the present, preventing anxiety about the future and remorse about the past from holding you back. This can interrupt the self-perpetuating cycle, allowing you to focus on positive and constructive actions.

Incorporating Relaxation Activities into Daily Routine

Integrating relaxation activities into your daily routine, even during non-anxious moments, can help regulate stress and prevent it from accumulating, thus breaking the cycle of anxiety.

Social Support

Talking to friends, family, or participating in support groups can provide the necessary support to break the cycle of anxiety. Sharing experiences and learning from others can be extremely helpful on the recovery journey.

Self-Care

Consistently practice self-care. Take time for yourself, engage in activities that make you feel good, and take care of your physical and emotional health. A healthy body and mind are more capable of breaking the cycle of anxiety.

The vicious cycle of anxiety is a complex trap, but it is not invincible. In the previous chapter, we explored in detail how anxiety can become a self-perpetuating cycle, fueled by interconnected thoughts, physical responses, and emotions. Understanding is the vital first step to overcoming this trap. Now, we turn to practical and accessible strategies to break this cycle, regain control, and work towards a more balanced and serene life.

The path to overcoming anxiety lies in self-management. In the next chapter, we will delve into valuable strategies to help you take control and reclaim inner peace. From daily practices to profound self-reflection techniques, we will learn to cultivate resilience and find peace amidst the storm of anxiety. These strategies are not just tools; they are invitations to a new way of living, with confidence and clarity.

8
SELF-MANAGEMENT STRATEGIES

*Be the conductor of your own calmness,
compose your melody, and harmonize your being.*

We live in a world of perpetual motion, brimming with demands, expectations, and challenges. In this scenario, it is common for anxiety to manifest itself, often becoming an unwelcome companion in our daily lives. Anxiety can range from mild to intense, impacting our quality of life and well-being. However, we are not destined to be captives of anxiety. We can develop practical and effective strategies to manage it and promote our own emotional equilibrium.

This chapter is a journey through the universe of anxiety self-management strategies. We will explore proven methods that can help alleviate anxiety and bring serenity into our lives. These are tools within our reach, waiting to be applied and integrated into our daily routine.

We will grasp the importance of acceptance, physical exercise, cognitive restructuring, and other practices that have proven effective in reducing anxiety levels. Additionally, we will delve into the realm of conscious breathing, progressive relaxation, and mindfulness, powerful techniques that connect us to the present and help us find inner peace.

By adopting these strategies, we are not merely combating the symptoms of anxiety. We are nurturing a resilient mindset, strengthening our ability to face challenges, and promoting our mental and physical health.

PRACTICAL STRATEGIES TO FACE MOMENTS OF HEIGHTENED ANXIETY

When faced with moments of heightened anxiety, possessing practical strategies to navigate these turbulent waters effectively and healthily is essential. Intense anxiety can manifest in various situations, from before a significant presentation to moments of great uncertainty. These are practical strategies that can help face such moments and regain control over our emotions:

Conscious Breathing (or Deep Breathing Technique)

Conscious breathing is a powerful tool to immediately alleviate anxiety. It helps calm the nervous system, reducing heart rate and blood pressure. A simple exercise involves inhaling slowly through the nose, counting to four, holding the breath for four seconds, and then exhaling through the mouth, counting again to four. Repeating this cycle a few times can bring immediate relief.

Practice of Acceptance and Commitment (ACT)

ACT is an approach that involves accepting thoughts and feelings without judgment, allowing them to pass through the mind without resisting them. Then, one commits to acting in accordance with personal values, even in the presence of these uncomfortable thoughts. This helps avoid fighting against anxiety, which often intensifies it.

Regular Physical Exercise

Regular physical exercise, such as walking, running, yoga, or dancing, releases endorphins, neurotransmitters that alleviate stress and anxiety. Moreover, exercise helps maintain a healthy sleep, which is crucial for anxiety control.

Mindfulness and Meditation Practice

Mindfulness and meditation can help calm the mind and cultivate awareness of the present moment. By focusing on breathing or a specific object, we can ward off anxious thoughts and find a state of calm and balance.

Setting Realistic Goals

Setting realistic and achievable goals helps reduce performance-related anxiety. Establishing specific, measurable, achievable, relevant, and time-bound goals (known as SMART goals) can provide a sense of control and diminish anxiety.

Progressive Muscle Relaxation Techniques

This technique involves intentionally contracting and relaxing muscle groups, starting from the feet and moving up to the head. This process helps release physical and mental tension, promoting a sense of relaxation.

Developing Relaxing Hobbies

Engaging in relaxing hobbies such as painting, gardening, cooking, or listening to music can provide a break from sources of stress and anxiety, allowing time for rest and rejuvenation.

Practice of Positive Self-Talk

Developing a positive and encouraging internal dialogue can help reverse negative thought patterns. Encouraging oneself with supportive words can shift perspective and reduce anxiety.

Adopting these practical strategies in moments of heightened anxiety can make a significant difference, empowering us to face challenges in a more balanced and resolute manner. Each person is unique, so it's important to experiment and discover which strategies work best for you. The key is for these practices to be aligned with your values and contribute to your mental health and well-being.

BREATHING, RELAXATION, AND MINDFULNESS TECHNIQUES FOR ANXIETY CONTROL

Mastering anxiety can be achieved through techniques of breathing, relaxation, and mindfulness. These strategies are effective in calming the mind, relieving stress, and aiding in the restoration of internal balance. Below, we shall delve into these practices and how they can be effectively applied:

Breathing Techniques

Breath is a potent tool for anxiety control, for it is intricately tied to our nervous system and emotional state. Utilizing breathing techniques can help calm the mind, reduce stress, and provide a sense of relaxation. Let us explore some of these techniques:

Diaphragmatic Breathing (or Abdominal Breathing): This technique involves deep breathing, filling the abdomen first and then the chest. As you inhale, the abdomen expands, and upon exhaling, it contracts. This helps to calm the nervous system and reduce anxiety.

How to:

1. Sit or lie down comfortably.
2. Place one hand on your chest and the other on your abdomen.
3. Inhale slowly through your nose, filling your abdomen first and then your chest.
4. Exhale through your mouth or nose, releasing the air from your chest and then your abdomen.

4-7-8 Breathing Pattern: In this pattern, you inhale through your nose counting to four, hold your breath for seven seconds, and then exhale through your mouth counting to eight. Repeat this cycle several times. It helps to calm the mind and induce sleep.

How to:

1. Close your eyes and place the tip of your tongue against the roof of your mouth, just behind your upper front teeth.
2. Exhale completely through your mouth, making a "whoosh" sound as the air leaves.
3. Close your mouth and inhale quietly through your nose to a mental count of four.
4. Hold your breath for a count of seven.
5. Exhale audibly through your mouth for a count of eight, making the "whoosh" sound again.

Alternate Nostril Breathing (Nadi Shodhana): It is a yogic breathing technique involving alternating nostrils during breathing, which balances the brain hemispheres, providing a calming effect.

How to:

1. Sit comfortably with an upright spine.
2. Use your thumb to close your right nostril and inhale slowly through the left nostril.
3. After a complete inhalation, close the left nostril with your ring finger and hold the breath for a few seconds.

4. Release the right nostril and exhale slowly through it.

5. Inhale through the right nostril, close it, and exhale through the left nostril.

6. Continue alternating in this manner.

These breathing techniques are invaluable tools for calming the mind and body during anxious moments. Practicing them regularly can enhance your stress response capability, providing tranquility and emotional balance. The choice of technique will depend on the situation and your personal preferences. Experiment with each and incorporate them into your routine to reap lasting benefits.

Relaxation Techniques

In addition to breathing techniques, various relaxation approaches can be highly effective in relieving anxiety and stress. These techniques aim to reduce muscle tension, calm the mind, and create a state of tranquility. Let's explore some of them:

Progressive Muscle Relaxation: This technique involves consciously contracting and then relaxing muscle groups, starting from the feet and moving up to the head. It helps release accumulated tension in the body.

How to:

1. Sit or lie down comfortably.
2. Begin by contracting the muscles of your feet for a few seconds and then completely relax them.

3. Proceed to gradually contract and relax each muscle group, moving from the feet to the head.

4. While contracting, feel the tension in the muscles, and while relaxing, feel the release of tension.

Guided Visualization: It involves imagining a relaxing environment or situation. You can create a peaceful scene in your mind and focus on it to reduce anxiety.

How to:

1. Find a quiet place and sit or lie down comfortably.
2. Close your eyes and take deep breaths to relax.
3. Create a soothing scene in your mind—it could be a beach, a forest, or any place that brings tranquility.
4. Visualize all the details of this scene, from colors to sounds and scents.

Biofeedback: It is a method that allows a person to learn to control bodily functions such as heart rate, blood pressure, and muscle tension. Through this feedback, one can learn to consciously relax.

How to:

1. Seek guidance from a specialized healthcare professional in biofeedback.
2. During a session, sensors will monitor your bodily functions.
3. With the guidance of the professional, you will learn techniques to control and reduce these functions.

These relaxation techniques are valuable for reducing anxiety, promoting well-being, and improving mental health. Incorporating these practices into your daily routine can make a significant difference in how you deal with stress and anxiety. Experiment with each and discover which suits your lifestyle and needs. Regular practice of these techniques can help achieve a state of calm and balance.

Mindfulness Practices

Mindfulness, an age-old practice rooted in Buddhist meditation, stands as a potent tool for managing anxiety. It entails complete and conscious attention to the present moment, allowing for a profound understanding of ourselves and the world around us. Let us delve into some mindfulness practices that can aid in reducing anxiety and promoting mental well-being:

Mindfulness Meditation: Mindfulness meditation stands as a foundational pillar of this practice. It necessitates dedicating time to focus on one's breath and the current moment. Sit in a comfortable position, pay keen attention to your breath, and when your mind begins to wander (as is natural), gently guide your focus back to your breath. This assists in calming the mind and fostering a state of tranquility.

Mindfulness of Body Sensations: This technique directs your attention toward the physical sensations of your body. Find a serene spot and attend to your body's sensations—the pressure against the chair, the sensation of the floor beneath your feet, the temperature of your skin. This aids in connecting with the present moment and dispelling anxious thoughts.

Non-Judgmental Observation of Thoughts: The non-judgmental observation of thoughts is a practice of acceptance. Instead of passing judgment or reacting emotionally to your thoughts, simply observe them. Acknowledge their presence, but refrain from emotional engagement. This can offer a clearer understanding of your thought patterns and assist in releasing the anxiety associated with them.

Throughout this chapter, we have delved into the depths of self-management strategies, becoming acquainted with valuable tools to confront and control anxiety. From the breathing techniques that aid us in finding calmness to the relaxation methods that alleviate accumulated tensions, each strategy is a vital piece in the puzzle of anxiety management.

Mindfulness, with its ability to keep us anchored in the present, and visualization, which transports us to peaceful environments, are powerful resources to balance our mind and body. Consistent practice of these techniques can truly transform our relationship with anxiety, offering us a heightened sense of calm, enhanced mental clarity, and a more balanced response to stress. Remember, the key lies in regular practice and the integration of these techniques into your routine to reap the long-term benefits.

In the next chapter, we will explore resilience, a fundamental skill for thriving amid the adversities that life presents. Resilience is not merely the capacity to withstand stress, but also the ability to adapt, learn, and grow from challenging experiences. Together, we shall discover how we can become more resilient, facing challenges with courage and transforming them into opportunities for our personal growth.

9

BUILDING RESILIENCE

Like a sturdy tree, bend with the storms,
but never break; grow, flourish, and blossom.

Life is a cycle of highs and lows, challenges and triumphs. Along our journey, we face unexpected turbulence, falls that take our breath away, and collisions that unsettle our emotional balance. In this universe of uncertainties and changes, resilience emerges as a vital anchor that keeps us steadfast, enabling us not only to survive but to thrive in the face of adversities.

Resilience is much more than weathering the storm. It is a masterful orchestration of our inner strength and ability to transform the negative into the positive, suffering into personal growth. It translates into the capacity to flex our minds and hearts to adapt, learn, and evolve from the challenges we face.

In this chapter, we will delve deeply into the construction of resilience, an inner journey of self-discovery and empowerment. We will learn how to cultivate this intrinsic quality, nourish it, and see it flourish within us and in our daily lives. Let us unravel the techniques and mindsets that aid us in becoming more resilient, in turning pain into wisdom, and adversity into growth.

THE NATURE OF RESILIENCE

Resilience is not a gift bestowed upon a fortunate few, but a skill that can be cultivated by all of us. It is the art of bending without breaking, of finding hope when all seems lost, and of emerging from the ashes with a renewed determination.

This inner strength empowers us to turn adversities into opportunities for growth. In the face of the most challenging situations, resilience allows us to find hope, learn from our falls, and emerge with renewed determination. It is a path of overcoming and self-improvement, where the scars of the past become the foundations for a more solid future.

DEVELOPING EMOTIONAL RESILIENCE

Resilience is a dynamic quality, a force that adapts, evolves, and strengthens over time. It is like a muscle that can be exercised and toned. The more we practice it, the more it develops, growing in intensity and depth.

Developing emotional resilience is an inner journey that requires self-exploration, awareness, and conscious action. It is a quality that, much like a muscle, can be fortified and refined over time. Let us delve deeply into the art of cultivating this crucial skill, where self-awareness and emotional acceptance play a fundamental role.

Self-Awareness and Emotional Acceptance

Resilience begins within us, in understanding and accepting our emotions. Understanding our own emotional patterns, triggers, and reactions is like mapping the emotional terrain we inhabit. Wholeheartedly accepting these emotions, even those we deem difficult or uncomfortable, is the first step in learning to handle them in a healthy manner. Recognizing that all emotions serve a purpose and are valid is an act of self-empathy that forms the foundation of our resilience.

A Strong Social Support Network

None of us is alone on this journey. Having a strong social support network is a fundamental pillar for emotional resilience. Friends, family, or support groups are precious sources of support in times of need. The ability to share our concerns, fears, and challenges with others creates a sense of belonging and alleviates the emotional burden we carry. By reaching out for help and offering help when possible, we are building essential bridges that strengthen us on the long path of life.

Cognitive Flexibility

Our way of interpreting and responding to events is a crucial aspect of emotional resilience. It is linked to our cognitive flexibility, which is the ability to adapt our way of thinking in the face of challenging situations. It is essential to be able to assess situations from different perspectives, question our beliefs, and adjust our responses according to the evolving reality. Cultivating a flexible and open mind helps us not to cling to limiting thought patterns, allowing us to find creative and constructive solutions to the challenges we face.

Setting Goals and Focusing on the Future

Establishing tangible and realistic goals is an effective way to give direction and purpose to our lives. Even the smallest goals can be powerful anchors for resilience. They help us maintain a sense of progress, believe in our potential, and provide a compass for our path. Focusing on the future, visualizing our goals, and believing we can achieve them, even in the face of difficulties, is an essential aspect of resilience. It is a constant reminder that there is light at the end of the tunnel, even in the darkest moments.

Physical Health and Well-being

Physical and emotional well-being are intricately intertwined. Maintaining a healthy lifestyle forms a solid foundation for emotional resilience. A balanced diet, regular physical exercise, and adequate sleep are pillars that fortify our body, which in turn supports our mind. Tending to our physical well-being is not just a matter of health; it is a vital strategy for building emotional resilience. A healthy body is the fertile soil in which our emotional resilience grows and flourishes.

These elements constitute the sturdy groundwork for the development of emotional resilience. It is an invitation to look inward, acknowledge our emotions, seek support, be flexible in our way of thinking, nurture our goals, and care for our body. Together, they guide us in constructing enduring resilience, strengthening us to face the storms of life and emerge stronger than ever.

HOW TO TURN ADVERSITY INTO PERSONAL GROWTH

The true magic of resilience emerges when we can transform adversity into personal growth. Let us delve into how we can find meaning in our struggles, learn from our failures, and emerge stronger after every storm. The ability to extract wisdom and maturity from our challenging experiences is the true essence of resilience.

Positive Reappraisal

Positive reappraisal is a powerful psychological strategy that helps us transform adversity into personal growth. Let us explore this transformative technique in more detail:

Interpreting Situations Positively: Positive reappraisal involves reinterpreting negative situations in a positive light. Rather than focusing solely on difficulties and disadvantages, we seek to identify the positive and meaningful aspects of the challenging experience.

Extracting Valuable Lessons: The practice of positive reappraisal enables us to extract valuable lessons from our challenging experiences. We can learn about our strengths and weaknesses, our values, and how to face similar situations more effectively in the future.

Building Resilience: By reevaluating adversity as a learning opportunity, we build resilience. This emotionally strengthens us to face future challenges, as we come to view each difficult situation as a stepping stone for our development.

Shifting the Internal Narrative: By altering how we interpret a setback, we can change our internal narrative. From a negative perspective, we can shift to seeing the situation as a chance for growth, realigning our view of ourselves and the world.

Finding Points of Light in Dark Situations: Positive reappraisal helps us find points of light even in the darkest situations. It could be an unexpected learning, a deeper connection with others, or a profound understanding of ourselves. These points of light provide us with hope and motivation to move forward.

Enhancing Emotional Well-being: By adopting a positive outlook, we experience an enhancement in emotional well-being. This can encompass increased happiness, reduced stress, and a sense of inner peace even in the face of adversity.

Application in Various Areas of Life: Positive reappraisal can be applied in various areas of life, such as relationships, career, health, and personal challenges. It is a versatile tool that assists us in facing life's vicissitudes with resilience and optimism.

In summary, positive reappraisal is a valuable skill that empowers us to turn challenges into opportunities.

It is a powerful mechanism of personal growth that helps us find meaning and strength in adverse experiences, enabling us to grow and flourish, regardless of circumstances.

Post-Traumatic Growth

Post-traumatic growth is a psychological phenomenon where an individual, after experiencing trauma or a highly stressful event, not only manages to recover emotionally but also grows and matures as a result of the experience. Let us delve into this remarkable ability to transform adversity into growth in detail:

Adversity as a Catalyst for Transformation: Trauma can act as a catalyst for profound transformation in a person's life. When facing highly stressful experiences, some individuals discover an inner strength previously unknown to them and develop a new purpose and perspective on life.

Shift in Perspective: Post-traumatic growth is often associated with a significant shift in perspective. The individual begins to see the world differently, placing greater value on the little things, interpersonal relationships, and life itself.

Appreciation of Life and Relationships: After trauma, there is a deeper appreciation for life and relationships. The individual may learn to appreciate everyday life, recognizing its fragility, while also cultivating more authentic and meaningful relationships.

Enhanced Resilience: Confronting and overcoming trauma can strengthen a person's resilience. They may develop more effective coping skills, aiding them in better dealing with future adversities and challenges.

Increased Empathy and Compassion: Trauma can sensitize a person to the suffering of others. They may develop greater empathy and compassion, transforming personal pain into motivation to help and support others.

Spiritual Growth: Some individuals experience spiritual growth after trauma, finding answers or meaning in spiritual dimensions of their lives. This can provide comfort and strength during the recovery journey.

Acceptance of Impermanence: Trauma can teach us to accept the impermanence of life and human frailty. This acceptance can lead to a more serene attitude towards life situations and an understanding that all things, good or bad, are temporary.

Development of New Life Goals: After trauma, a person may reformulate their life goals and objectives. They may adopt a new direction, often more aligned with their authentic values and desires.

Post-traumatic growth illustrates the remarkable human resilience and the ability to transform even the most devastating experiences into opportunities for growth and strength. By learning from the past and cultivating a more positive and compassionate outlook, it is possible to emerge from trauma not only surviving but truly growing and thriving.

Enhancing Resilience Through Adversity

Facing and overcoming adversities is a journey that can enhance our resilience and strengthen our character. Each challenge presents a valuable opportunity for us to grow and develop important skills. Let us explore in more detail how adversity can become a means of growth and development:

Development of Resilience: Resilience is the ability to adapt and recover after experiencing challenges and adversities. Adversity offers the opportunity to strengthen this vital skill, helping us face future challenges with more confidence.

Learning and Adaptation: Each challenge brings valuable lessons with it. We can learn from our mistakes and difficulties, adapting to circumstances and adjusting our approach for future similar situations.

Expanding Emotional Skills: Adversity often puts us in touch with a wide range of emotions. Learning to recognize, understand, and manage these emotions is a crucial part of personal growth that can make us more emotionally intelligent and resilient.

Cultivation of Determination and Perseverance: Facing adversities challenges us to persist and maintain determination, even in the face of obstacles. This cultivation of perseverance can strengthen our mindset and help us achieve our long-term goals.

Building Autonomy: Adversity often places us in situations where we need to make decisions and take responsibility for our actions. This can promote the development of autonomy and confidence in our abilities.

Fostering Personal Growth: By overcoming challenges, we can grow personally in various ways, such as increasing our self-awareness, strengthening our values, and finding a deeper purpose in our lives.

Problem-Solving Skills: Adversity challenges us to solve problems in innovative and effective ways. We develop problem-solving skills that can be applied in various areas of our lives.

Strengthening Relationships: Facing challenges can create an opportunity to strengthen our relationships. Sharing difficult experiences with friends, family, or support groups can create deeper connections.

Adversity is not just a trial; it is a demanding teacher that challenges us to grow and enhance our skills. When we face challenges constructively and learn from them, we are preparing ourselves for a more resilient and rewarding future. The journey on the path of resilience begins with recognizing the growth potential that each challenge presents.

Acceptance of Impermanence

Acceptance of impermanence is a powerful life philosophy that acknowledges that everything is subject to constant change. Let us deepen our understanding of this concept and how it can positively influence our approach to life:

Concept of Impermanence: Impermanence is the transient and mutable nature of all things. Nothing remains unchanged and eternal; everything is subject to change, from the simplest events to the grand phases of life.

Balance Amidst Changes: Embracing impermanence aids in balancing our emotions and attitudes towards change. Instead of resisting or fearing change, we learn to flow with it, maintaining our inner serenity.

Cultivation of Acceptance: Accepting impermanence involves cultivating an attitude of acceptance towards the natural flow of life. It means embracing every moment, regardless of being positive or negative, as part of life's journey.

Reduction of Suffering: Resistance to impermanence can lead to suffering. Embracing it helps reduce this suffering, as we understand that happiness and sadness are temporary, and that the very nature of life is cyclical.

Mindset of Healthy Detachment: Grasping impermanence leads to a mindset of healthy detachment. We do not excessively cling to anything, knowing that everything can change. This liberates the mind from the clutches of fear and anxiety.

Resilience in the Face of Changes: Accepting impermanence aids in developing resilience. We become better prepared to deal with the changes and challenges life presents, knowing that the current situation is just a phase and can be surpassed.

Cultivation of Appreciation: Knowing that nothing lasts forever, we learn to appreciate each present moment more. We value the good experiences and learn from adversities, understanding that they are all part of the natural flow of life.

Spirituality and Philosophy of Life: Acceptance of impermanence is a foundational principle in many spiritual traditions and life philosophies. It encourages the pursuit of inner peace, wisdom, and compassion.

Peace in the Present Moment: By embracing impermanence, we find peace in the present moment. We are not preoccupied with the past or the future, knowing that each moment is unique and valuable in its own essence.

The practice of accepting impermanence helps us live with more grace and flexibility, allowing our life journey to flow naturally. We find contentment in the present, regardless of what the future may bring, and embrace change as an inevitable and enriching part of our existence.

Cultivating Resilience in Everyday Life

Resilience is a valuable skill that helps us face life's challenges with strength and adaptability. Let us explore practical ways to cultivate resilience in our daily lives to better prepare ourselves for difficult times:

Self-Awareness and Self-Management: Understanding our emotions, thoughts, and reactions is the first step in cultivating resilience. By being self-aware, we can effectively manage our emotions during challenges.

Setting Realistic Goals: Defining realistic and achievable goals helps us stay focused and motivated. Achieving these goals strengthens our belief in our ability to face challenges.

Developing Problem-Solving Skills: We learn to approach problems in a structured and effective manner, seeking constructive solutions. This skill is fundamental to addressing challenges productively.

Building a Support Network: Cultivating positive and supportive relationships is crucial. Having a network of friends, family, or colleagues with whom we can share our challenges provides valuable support.

Practicing Gratitude and Contentment: Focusing on what we have and expressing gratitude helps maintain a positive perspective. This emotionally strengthens us to face difficult moments.

Adopting a Healthy Lifestyle: A balanced diet, regular physical exercise, and good quality sleep are essential for resilience. A healthy body helps maintain a balanced and resilient mind.

Cultivating Hobbies and Interests: Engaging in activities we are passionate about can be a great relief from daily stress and pressure. These activities offer an outlet and an opportunity to renew our energy.

Fostering Mental Flexibility: Life is uncertain, and often things don't go as planned. Learning to adapt and be flexible in various situations is a key attribute of resilience.

Pursuing Continuous Learning: Being open to learning and growth is vital. Each experience, whether good or bad, teaches us something. Extracting lessons from challenges makes us stronger.

Practicing Mindfulness and Meditation: Meditation and mindfulness practice can help calm the mind and strengthen our ability to deal with stress and adversity.

Maintaining a Positive Attitude: Maintaining a positive attitude even in difficult times can make a significant difference. Optimism helps us face challenges with resilience and determination.

Acknowledging and Accepting Emotions: Accepting and processing our emotions, even the negative ones, is fundamental. This helps us not get overwhelmed and develop a deeper understanding of ourselves.

Cultivating resilience in everyday life not only helps us face immediate challenges but also strengthens us to face future challenges with more confidence and balance. It's a proactive approach to living a fulfilling and meaningful life, regardless of circumstances.

In this chapter, we delve deep into emotional resilience, exploring how it can be cultivated and nurtured over time. Resilience is not an innate quality but rather an ability we can foster and strengthen. We have discovered that self-awareness, robust support networks, cognitive flexibility, goal setting, and physical well-being form the bedrock of resilience.

Furthermore, we engage in a discussion on how the true enchantment of resilience is unveiled when we transform adversity into personal growth. Positive reassessment, post-traumatic growth, and the ability to enhance our resilience through adversity constitute the pillars of this transformative process.

Now, as we conclude our journey of resilience building, we stand ready to venture forth and explore how our lifestyle and well-being play a crucial role in our mental and emotional health. The upcoming chapter will guide us on a path toward choices and habits that foster lasting happiness, balance, and mental well-being. We shall learn how to nurture our body and mind to construct a fulfilling and meaningful life.

10

LIFESTYLE AND WELL-BEING

Every choice is a blank canvas; paint your picture of peace, coloring your life with well-being.

The lifestyle we choose and the practices we incorporate daily have a profound impact on our physical and mental health. From the food we choose to the way we manage stress, each decision shapes our quality of life and our ability to cope with anxiety.

Throughout this chapter, we will delve into practical strategies to promote a healthier and less anxious lifestyle. We will address the importance of a balanced diet and physical exercise, providing insights into how these fundamental elements can be powerful allies in anxiety management.

Discover how small changes in your daily routine, conscious choices regarding nutrition, and regular physical activities can make a significant difference in your journey toward emotional and physical well-being.

STRATEGIES TO PROMOTE A HEALTHIER, LESS ANXIOUS LIFESTYLE

Promoting a healthy and less anxious lifestyle is a commitment to oneself to cultivate well-being in all areas of life. These are practical strategies that will help you achieve this desired balance.

Regular Practice of Physical Exercise

Physical activity is a powerful ally in the quest for a less anxious life. Whether through a morning run, a revitalizing yoga class, or a simple walk in the park, exercise releases endorphins, neurotransmitters responsible for the sensation of well-being. Incorporate a physical activity that brings you joy into your daily routine and enjoy the benefits both physically and mentally.

Meditation and Relaxation Practices

Meditating and practicing relaxation techniques such as deep breathing and mindfulness are like balms for the anxious mind. Dedicate a few minutes every day to disconnect from the external world and connect with yourself. By calming the mind and slowing down, you will find clarity and inner peace.

Balanced Diet

Our diet plays a fundamental role in our mental health. Opt for a balanced and nutritious diet, consisting of fruits, vegetables, whole grains, lean proteins, and healthy fats. Avoid processed foods, excess sugar, and caffeine, as they can trigger or exacerbate anxiety symptoms.

Quality Sleep

Sleep is a crucial component for mental health. Establish a consistent sleep routine, create a conducive sleep environment, and avoid stimulants before bedtime. Restorative sleep helps renew the body and mind, strengthening your ability to face the day with tranquility.

Stress Management

Mastering stress is a valuable skill for a less anxious life. Organize your time effectively, learn to delegate tasks, and practice relaxation techniques. Know when to say no and reserve time for activities that relax you.

Leisure Activities

Allow yourself leisure moments dedicated to activities you love. Painting, reading, gardening, music, or any hobby that disconnects you from daily worries serves as an escape valve for stress and anxiety.

Establishing a Structured Routine

Set up a well-structured daily routine, including schedules for meals, exercise, work, leisure, and sleep. Predictability and organization can help reduce anxiety, providing a sense of control.

Fostering Social Relationships

Cultivating healthy and meaningful relationships is essential for emotional well-being. Share your experiences with friends and family, participate in groups with common interests, and offer your support to others. Social support can alleviate anxiety and create a safety net.

Learning and Personal Growth

Investing in your personal development is a step toward a more fulfilled and less anxious life. Set achievable goals that motivate you to grow and develop. The continuous pursuit of learning and growth provides a sense of purpose and satisfaction.

Gratitude and Cultivation of Optimism

Daily gratitude practice is a powerful antidote to anxiety. Recognize the positive aspects of your life and express gratitude for them. Cultivating an optimistic perspective, focusing on solutions rather than problems, will transform your approach to life and contribute to anxiety reduction.

By implementing these strategies into your daily life, you will be building a healthier and less anxious lifestyle, promoting an essential balance between body, mind, and spirit. Remember that well-being is an ongoing journey, and every step you take toward a healthier lifestyle is a step toward a more fulfilling and peaceful life.

THE IMPORTANCE OF A BALANCED DIET AND PHYSICAL EXERCISE IN MANAGING ANXIETY

We live in an era where the fast pace of everyday life often leaves us trapped in a cycle of stress and anxiety. Amidst this challenging reality, recognizing the significance of a balanced diet and regular physical exercise is fundamental to maintain not only our physical health but also our mental well-being.

Impact of Diet on Anxiety

The relationship between diet and anxiety is profound. Foods rich in simple sugars and trans fats can trigger blood sugar fluctuations, affecting mood and increasing anxiety. On the other hand, a diet rich in fruits, vegetables, whole grains, and lean proteins can provide the necessary nutrients for mental balance.

Serotonin, a neurotransmitter associated with well-being and mood, can be influenced by diet. Tryptophan, an amino acid precursor to serotonin, can be found in foods such as nuts, seeds, legumes, and fish, and incorporating them into your diet can help regulate mood and anxiety.

Benefits of Physical Exercise on Anxiety

Physical exercise is one of the most effective ways to reduce anxiety. During physical activities, our body releases endorphins, brain chemicals that act as natural painkillers and mood stabilizers. Furthermore, exercise helps reduce cortisol production, the stress hormone.

In addition to the chemical impact, regular exercise is directly related to better sleep quality, something essential for anxiety control. Adequate sleep restores the body and mind, preparing us to face the day with calmness and mental clarity.

Incorporating a Balanced Diet and Exercise into Your Routine

Incorporating a balanced diet and physical exercise into our routine may seem challenging initially, but it is entirely achievable with a gradual and consistent approach. Start by making small changes to your diet, introducing more healthy foods and reducing harmful ones. Likewise, try different types of exercises until you find the ones that please you and fit into your life.

Consulting a nutritionist or a healthcare professional is an excellent way to get specific guidance on a balanced diet that meets your needs. For exercises, considering guidance from a personal trainer for a personalized plan can be a great option.

The Quest for Balance

Finding the right balance between a balanced diet and regular physical exercise is an individual quest. Each person is unique, and their needs vary. Experiment with different approaches, listen to your body, and make adjustments as needed. Keep in mind that excessive pressure to drastically change your diet or exercise intensely can increase anxiety. Consistency and moderation are key to achieving and maintaining a healthy lifestyle.

By prioritizing a balanced diet and regular physical exercise, you are making a valuable investment in your physical and mental health. These conscious choices can play a significant role in anxiety control and the pursuit of a fulfilling and balanced life. So, move forward, adopt healthy habits, and enjoy the lasting benefits they can provide for your well-being.

In this chapter, we have explored the vital importance of a balanced lifestyle in facing anxiety. We have observed that our diet and physical activity have a profound impact not only on our physical health but also on our mental well-being. A balanced diet, rich in essential nutrients, combined with regular physical exercise, can be a great ally in the pursuit of a less anxious and more fulfilling life.

Keep in mind that it's not about seeking perfection, but rather balance. It's about making conscious choices, gradually incorporating positive changes into our daily routine. By taking care of our body, we are also nurturing our mind. By integrating healthy eating and physical activity into our everyday life, we are taking concrete steps towards a state of balance and well-being.

In the next chapter, we will delve into an increasingly prevalent topic in our lives: technology. In a digitized and interconnected world, technology can have a significant impact on our mental health, including anxiety. We will explore how excessive use of devices, social media, and constant exposure to the digital world can affect our emotional health. Additionally, we will discuss strategies and practices that allow us to use technology consciously and beneficially for our mental health, seeking a healthy balance between online and offline life.

11

TECHNOLOGY AND ANXIETY

Master the art of digital presence, balancing it with the serenity of the real world.

We live in an era where technology permeates every aspect of our lives. From waking to slumber, we are constantly immersed in the digital realm. Technological innovations have opened doors to greater connectivity, efficiency, and convenience. However, this digital revolution has also brought forth a set of challenges, particularly concerning our mental well-being. In this chapter, we will delve into the realm of technology and its influence on anxiety.

Instant connectivity and uninterrupted access to information have their advantages but also bring a host of concerns for mental health. Anxiety, one of the most prevalent issues in our modern world, is heavily impacted by the excessive and improper use of technology. We will explore how unrestrained information consumption, the pressure of social networks, digital isolation, and dependency on electronic devices are interconnected with anxiety.

Throughout this chapter, we will examine the direct impact of excessive technology use on our mental health. We will analyze how digital information overload, constant comparison, lack of face-to-face interaction, and its influence on sleep quality can contribute to anxiety and stress. Understanding these effects is essential to take significant steps towards a healthy balance between technology and our emotional well-being.

In addition to identifying the challenges, we will also present practical and effective strategies to mitigate the detrimental effects of excessive technology use. After all, technology is not inherently negative; its conscious and balanced use can be beneficial. We will discuss the importance of setting clear boundaries, practicing digital detachment, creating space for unplugged activities, and cultivating digital awareness. These practices can help us regain control over our relationship with technology and, consequently, alleviate the anxiety associated with it.

THE IMPACT OF EXCESSIVE TECHNOLOGY USE ON ANXIETY

The pervasive presence and ubiquitous use of technology in contemporary society have brought forth a vast spectrum of changes and profound impacts across various spheres of human life. However, one of these impacts deserving special attention is the effect of excessive technology use on anxiety, a condition that affects millions of people worldwide.

Information Overload and Digital Stress

The digital age has ushered in an incessant deluge of information. We are exposed to an avalanche of news, social media updates, emails, instant messages, and app notifications every second. While the ease of information access is a blessing, information overload can be overwhelming. The resulting digital stress from this information excess can lead to anxiety and exhaustion. The difficulty in discerning what is important and relevant amidst this avalanche can create a sense of despair and lack of control, fueling anxiety.

Social Comparison and Insecurity

Social networks, despite providing a platform for connection and sharing, often serve as stages for social comparison. Exposure to others' seemingly perfect lives can foster feelings of inadequacy and low self-esteem. People tend to compare their lives, appearances, achievements, and successes with others, engendering a constant and often unrealistic competition. This can lead to anxiety, as individuals feel pressured to meet unattainable standards.

Isolation and Reduced Face-to-Face Interactivity

While we are more digitally interconnected, this does not necessarily translate into greater emotional and social connection. Virtual interactions, often impersonal and superficial, are replacing deeper and more meaningful face-to-face interactions. The resulting emotional isolation can lead to loneliness and anxiety. The lack of genuine and profound human contact can leave individuals feeling disconnected and anxious, despite their seemingly vast presence on social media.

Impact on Sleep Quality

The habit of using electronic devices before bedtime is common in the digital age. However, exposure to the blue light emitted by these devices can disrupt our sleep cycle. Sleep quality is essential for mental health, and its disruption due to excessive technology use is closely linked to increased anxiety and stress. Inadequate sleep can heighten vulnerability to stress and diminish the ability to manage daily pressures, thereby amplifying anxiety.

These are merely a few of the detrimental effects of excessive technology use on anxiety, underscoring the pressing need to address and mitigate these impacts to preserve our mental health and well-being.

STRATEGIES TO BALANCE TECHNOLOGY USE AND REDUCE OVERLOAD

We dwell in a digital era where technology has seamlessly woven itself into the fabric of our lives. However, striking a harmonious balance between this constant presence and a balanced, healthy life is crucial for our mental well-being. Here are strategies that can aid in balancing technology use and alleviating the associated overload:

Establish Clear Boundaries

Set clear limits for technology use in your daily routine. Define specific times for online activities and tech-free periods, such as during meals and before sleep. These boundaries help deter excessive use and foster a healthier relationship with devices.

Blocking Harmful People and Topics

Leverage the available tools on social media and applications to block individuals and topics that act as triggers for anxiety. Shielding oneself from negative content is a significant way to care for your mental health.

Practice Digital Detox

Take regular breaks to completely disconnect. This could be a few hours during the day or certain days of the week. Utilize this time to re-engage with offline activities and with yourself. Digital detox is essential to alleviate the stress and anxiety associated with constant technological exposure.

Carve Out Space for Disconnected Activities

Allocate time for hobbies and activities that do not involve electronic devices. This might include outdoor exercises, reading physical books, art, or any activity that allows disconnection from the digital world. These moments of disconnection are vital for our mental health and well-being.

Exercise Digital Awareness

Be mindful of how you use technology. Before opening an app or website, ask yourself if it's truly necessary at that moment. Limit yourself to apps and information that are useful and relevant to your life. Avoiding automatic use of technology can reduce stress and anxiety.

Encourage Face-to-Face Interactions

Prioritize personal contact and offline social interactions whenever possible. Make time to be with friends and family, engage in social events, and participate in community activities. Face-to-face interactions are crucial for our mental and emotional well-being.

Attend to Your Mental Health

Keep a vigilant eye on your mental well-being. If you notice that technology use is adversely affecting your anxiety or mental health, seek professional help from a psychologist or therapist. It is fundamental to care for our mental health to navigate the challenges related to technology.

Establish a Tranquil Space

Create a space in your home where technology is not allowed. This is a place where you can completely disconnect and dedicate yourself to peace and tranquility. Having a technology-free zone helps find moments of serenity amidst digital bustle.

Practice Mindful Breathing

When you feel that technology is inducing anxiety, take a few minutes for mindful breathing. Inhale deeply, hold for a few seconds, and exhale slowly. This can help calm the mind and reduce the anxiety associated with excessive technology use.

While technology has brought incredible advancements, its constant presence in our lives can also trigger anxiety, stress, and other emotional challenges. In this chapter, we examined how information overload, social comparison, isolation, and the impact on sleep quality can contribute to anxiety in a digital world.

However, we also provided a comprehensive set of strategies to balance technology use and reduce overload. These strategies include setting clear boundaries, blocking harmful content, digital detoxing, creating space for offline activities, digital awareness, valuing personal interactions, caring for mental health, establishing a calm environment, and practicing mindful breathing.

By embracing these strategies and cultivating a mindful relationship with technology, we can face the challenges of the digital era in a more balanced way, promoting our mental health and well-being.

In the next chapter, we will delve into a fundamental area for our emotional well-being: relationships and social support. Our interactions with friends, family, and communities play a crucial role in our mental health. We will explore how building and maintaining healthy relationships can help reduce anxiety, provide emotional support, and create a safety net during challenging times.

12

RELATIONSHIPS AND SOCIAL SUPPORT

In every connection, we find strength; together we are a symphony, harmony in the battle against anxiety.

We live in an interconnected world, where our lives are interwoven by the relationships we forge along the way. Each connection, be it with friends, family, colleagues, or even strangers, contributes to the intricate tapestry of our lives.

Relationships are not mere superficial interactions; they are the backbone of our existence. From the close bonds with those who share our daily lives to the fleeting encounters that remind us of our shared humanity, relationships shape our emotional world. And as we explore the intricate intersection of these connections and our anxiety, we seek to understand how our interpersonal interactions can alleviate or exacerbate the burden of worry and fear.

In this chapter, we delve deep into the intricacies of human relationships. We investigate how emotional support can be a bulwark against anxiety, how lack of connections can fuel loneliness and insecurity, and how empathy and understanding can be beacons of light in the darkest moments. In our journey, we discover that while positive relationships can nourish our soul and empower us to face the world, toxic ones can undermine our confidence and sow doubt in our hearts.

In addition to examining the influence of relationships on our anxiety, we also present powerful strategies to nurture and strengthen these crucial connections. From transparent communication to seeking professional help when needed, we are about to unveil the arsenal of tools available to build healthy relationships and seek the emotional support we all require.

THE INFLUENCE OF RELATIONSHIPS ON ANXIETY

The bonds we forge with others throughout our lives are not merely social connections; they are threads that weave the tapestry of our mental well-being. In our quest to comprehend the intricate relationship between relationships and anxiety, we unravel the substantial impact they can have on our emotional state. From providing comforting relief to exacerbating our fears, relationships shape our experiences of anxiety in profound and varied ways. Let us examine how relationships can influence our anxiety:

Emotional Support and Anxiety Reduction

Healthy relationships, built on trust, respect, and mutual support, have the power to function as true antidotes to anxiety. Having someone we can trust wholeheartedly, with whom we can share our deepest anxieties and fears, is a balm for anxiety. Emotional support gives us the assurance that we are not alone in our challenges, enabling us to face them with greater resilience and hope. The empathy and encouragement we receive in meaningful relationships can calm the inner storm, providing a safe harbor for our distress.

Toxic Relationships and Aggravation of Anxiety

Just as positive relationships can offer solace, toxic relationships have the opposite effect: intensifying our levels of anxiety. Environments where there is a lack of support, understanding, or worse, emotional or physical abuse, can be cauldrons of stress and anxiety. Identifying and subsequently distancing ourselves from these detrimental relationships is essential to safeguard our mental health. Ending toxic relationships is an act of self-compassion and a crucial step toward a more stable and calm emotional state.

Loneliness and Anxiety

Loneliness can be fertile ground for the growth of anxiety. The absence of meaningful social interactions and emotional connections can lead to a profound sense of isolation, which in turn can trigger anxiety. It is vital, therefore, to cultivate healthy relationships and invest time and effort in building genuine connections. These relationships can act as bulwarks against loneliness and its detrimental effects on our mental health.

Empathy and Understanding as Relief for Anxiety

Relationships characterized by empathy, understanding, and open and effective communication can provide valuable relief for anxiety. The feeling of being truly understood and heard, without judgment, can alleviate the burden of anxiety. In these relationships, we find a safe space to express our most intimate thoughts and emotions, which can have a reassuring effect on our restless minds.

STRATEGIES TO CULTIVATE HEALTHY RELATIONSHIPS AND SEEK EMOTIONAL SUPPORT

Cultivating healthy relationships and seeking emotional support are crucial skills for enhancing our mental well-being and effectively confronting anxiety. Let us explore strategies that can assist us in strengthening our interpersonal connections and seeking the necessary support when needed:

Clear and Empathetic Communication

Communication is the bedrock of any healthy relationship. The ability to express our feelings, needs, and concerns clearly and respectfully is crucial. Moreover, actively listening to what others have to say, demonstrating empathy and understanding, can prevent misunderstandings that often turn into sources of anxiety. Clear and empathetic communication is the cornerstone for building strong and healthy connections.

Establishment of Healthy Boundaries

Setting healthy boundaries is a demonstration of self-love and mutual respect. The ability to say 'no' when necessary and set clear limits on what is acceptable and what is not in a relationship is fundamental. This helps maintain a balanced dynamic, preventing the stress and anxiety that come from disrespect or overload. Establishing boundaries is a form of self-care and is essential for lasting and healthy relationships.

Expression of Gratitude and Appreciation

Expressing gratitude and appreciation is a powerful way to strengthen interpersonal bonds. Acknowledging the positive contributions of people in our lives creates an environment of positivity and harmony. Gratitude promotes a virtuous cycle of emotional well-being, strengthening our relationships and contributing to a more balanced and less anxious mental state.

Empathy and Active Understanding

Empathy is one of the most valuable qualities we can cultivate in our relationships. Putting ourselves in others' shoes, striving to understand their feelings and perspectives, is a powerful gesture. Active understanding shows care and genuine interest, creating an emotionally nourishing environment and reducing anxiety by providing a safe space to express our emotions.

Encouragement of Personal Growth

Healthy relationships not only accept but also encourage personal growth. Encouraging and supporting the goals and aspirations of others lays a foundation for lasting and fulfilling relationships. When we support the growth of people in our lives, we are building a community where everyone has the opportunity to develop and reach their fullest potential.

Seeking Professional Help

When anxiety becomes overwhelming and begins to impair our quality of life, seeking professional help is a crucial step. Psychologists, therapists, and counselors are available to offer specialized guidance and strategies for dealing with anxiety. Moreover, these professionals can assist us in improving our relationships, providing crucial support for our mental health.

Participation in Social and Community Activities

Engaging in social and community activities is an excellent way to create and strengthen meaningful relationships. Connecting to a larger group and contributing to the community not only creates new friendships but also provides a sense of purpose and meaning. Involvement in common causes and contributing to the well-being of the community can reduce anxiety, strengthening our mental health.

Cultivation of Positive Family Relationships

Family ties are a crucial pillar in our lives. Strengthening these connections is an essential part of cultivating healthy relationships. Investing time and effort in maintaining a positive relationship with family members can be a significant source of emotional support. A united and loving family can be a haven in times of anxiety, offering comfort and emotional support.

In this chapter, we have explored the profound influence relationships have on our anxiety and how they can be both a source of emotional support and a source of stress. We have learned that when cultivated in a healthy manner, relationships can play a fundamental role in reducing anxiety by providing emotional support, empathy, and understanding. At the same time, we have identified the importance of establishing boundaries and recognizing toxic relationships that can worsen anxiety.

The strategies discussed in this chapter, such as clear communication, empathy, setting healthy boundaries, and pursuing personal growth, provide practical tools to improve our relationships and, consequently, our mental health.

As we move forward, we are reminded that our connections with others are a valuable resource for confronting anxiety and finding emotional support. By cultivating healthy relationships and implementing these strategies, we take significant steps toward a life with less anxiety and more emotional balance.

In the next chapter, we will delve into the importance of seeking professional help when facing anxiety. We will explore the various resources available, from psychologists and therapists to therapeutic approaches, that can provide specialized guidance and effective strategies for dealing with anxiety. Seeking professional help is a crucial step for many individuals facing emotional challenges, and this chapter will provide valuable insights on how to take this important step towards mental well-being.

13

SEEKING PROFESSIONAL HELP

In the quest for illumination, find courage; within the voice of the professional, uncover your path to healing.

The journey of anxiety is an intricate path, often challenging, teeming with emotional peaks and valleys, tumultuous thoughts, and uncertainties that can obscure the horizon of mental well-being. Anxiety can manifest in various ways and intensities, affecting our ability to savor life and fulfill our daily responsibilities. It is an emotional state that should not be underestimated, for it can undermine our quality of life and interfere with our social interactions, work, and personal relations.

It is crucial to acknowledge that facing anxiety alone can be overwhelming and often ineffective. At times, the support of friends and family may not suffice to provide the tools and strategies needed to overcome the barriers that anxiety imposes on our lives. It is at this point that seeking professional help becomes pivotal in steering towards emotional well-being.

This chapter is dedicated to understanding the significance of seeking professional assistance, including psychologists and psychiatrists, on the journey to overcome anxiety. We will delve into the reasons why expert guidance can make a substantial difference, not only in alleviating symptoms but also in a deeper comprehension of the roots of anxiety. We will demystify the taboos that often surround therapy, encouraging a more mindful and informed approach to seeking professional assistance.

THE SIGNIFICANCE OF SEEKING PROFESSIONAL HELP

Anxiety is an intricate condition that can manifest in various forms and intensities, impacting life in diverse ways. As anxiety becomes more prevalent and impactful, seeking professional help becomes a vital necessity. Here are some reasons why the assistance of psychologists and psychiatrists is paramount:

In-Depth Understanding of Anxiety

Mental health professionals possess the knowledge and experience required to delve into the understanding of anxiety. They can diagnose anxiety and identify the specific triggers that manifest in each case. With this deeper comprehension, personalized and effective coping strategies can be developed.

Development of Personalized Strategies

As each individual grapples with anxiety in unique ways, a personalized treatment plan is essential to address the specific needs and challenges of each person. Mental health professionals can devise tailor-made strategies that encompass therapies, relaxation exercises, coping techniques, and in some cases, medication.

Access to Specialized Therapeutic Techniques

Mental health professionals have access to a broad range of proven therapeutic techniques that can be highly effective in anxiety treatment. These techniques encompass Cognitive-Behavioral Therapy (CBT), Mindfulness, Acceptance and Commitment Therapy (ACT), and many other approaches that can provide relief and furnish valuable tools to manage anxiety.

Provision of Professional Support

Professional support is crucial in dealing with anxiety. Psychologists and psychiatrists are trained not only to provide guidance and strategies but also to offer emotional support. Having a professional by your side can make a significant difference in your journey to overcome anxiety.

Prevention and Crisis Management

Mental health professionals are trained to recognize signs of an impending crisis and assist in preventing it. They can aid in creating safety plans and strategies to avoid relapses or minimize their impact. This is particularly important for individuals experiencing chronic anxiety or anxiety disorders.

Ultimately, seeking professional help for anxiety is not only a display of self-sufficiency but also a courageous step towards a more balanced and happier life. Each person is unique, and the assistance of a psychologist or psychiatrist can provide the necessary support to effectively and empoweringly face the challenges of anxiety.

DEMYSTIFYING TABOOS SURROUNDING THERAPY

It is important to debunk the misconceptions and taboos surrounding therapy, as these misguided notions can deter people from seeking the support they need for their mental well-being. Let's explore some of these myths:

Therapy is not a Sign of Weakness

One of the most common and detrimental taboos associated with therapy is the belief that seeking help from a professional is a sign of weakness. However, this couldn't be farther from the truth. Seeking help is a sign of strength and courage. It is a demonstration of self-sufficiency and determination to improve one's mental health. Acknowledging that everyone faces emotional challenges at some point in life and that seeking support is an intelligent and assertive decision is an essential step in dispelling this taboo.

Therapy is not Solely for Severe Issues

Another common misconception is that therapy is reserved only for individuals with severe mental health problems. However, therapy is beneficial for anyone dealing with stress, anxiety, relationship issues, life transitions, or seeking self-awareness. It is a powerful tool to promote emotional well-being in a variety of situations. Everyone deserves to take care of their mental health, regardless of the severity of the issue.

Therapy is not an Endless Process

Some may fear that once they start therapy, they will be stuck in that process forever. However, therapy is an adaptable and flexible process. The goal is to provide the necessary tools for you to sustain yourself emotionally. Therapists are there to help you achieve your goals and determine when you are ready to move forward, providing autonomy and continuous progress. Therapy aims to empower you to face future challenges independently and confidently.

Therapy is not Solely About Discussing Problems

Therapy goes beyond merely talking about your problems. It is a safe and confidential environment to explore your emotions, behaviors, and thoughts in depth. Therapists provide guidance, teach coping skills, assist in developing strategies to deal with life's challenges more effectively, and promote self-discovery. Therapy is a space for personal growth and emotional development, paving the way for a more balanced and meaningful life.

Seeking professional help to address anxiety is a crucial step towards a more balanced and healthy life. This chapter has explored the importance of seeking assistance from psychologists and psychiatrists, emphasizing that this search is not a sign of weakness, but rather a display of strength and determination to care for mental health. We have debunked the taboos associated with therapy, underscoring that it is not solely for severe problems and does not represent an endless process. Therapy is a space for growth, where strategies are developed, and a profound understanding of anxiety is attained.

Mental health professionals offer not only emotional support but also specialized therapeutic techniques to treat anxiety. Through a personalized process, they assist in identifying triggers and constructing strategies tailored to the unique needs of each individual. Additionally, they provide support to prevent and manage crises, essential for those dealing with chronic anxiety or related disorders.

By dispelling misconceptions and encouraging the pursuit of professional help, we hope to have inspired considering therapy as a valuable tool to address anxiety. Through it, one can achieve a more fulfilling and balanced life, promoting emotional well-being and enhancing the quality of life. The journey to overcome anxiety is a path of courage, self-awareness, and growth, and professional help can be a valuable guide on this journey.

CONCLUSION

As we reach the conclusion of this journey through 'Anxiety, Inc.', it is crucial to reiterate and underscore the significance of resolutely facing anxiety in our lives. Anxiety, with its profound and often intricate ramifications, can shape our experiences and our perception of the world. However, it is fundamental to remember that we are not defenseless against this condition. Every page of this book has been a call to action, an invitation to confront anxiety head-on and not allow it to dominate us.

The central message of this book is one of hope and encouragement. It is possible to live a fulfilling life, even in the presence of anxiety. It is not an insurmountable obstacle but a challenge that, with the right approach, can be managed and overcome. The journey towards emotional balance and inner peace can begin with a simple step: seeking help.

Keep in mind that you are not alone; many people face anxiety, and there is a support network available, from friends and family to mental health professionals, who are willing to assist. Having the courage to confront anxiety is an act of self-compassion and self-investment.

The path may be challenging, with ups and downs, but every step you take towards managing anxiety is a step towards a healthier, more balanced, and fulfilled life. Remember that anxiety does not define who you are; it is merely a part of your experience. With determination, effective strategies, and support, you can gain greater control over anxiety and achieve a more meaningful and joyful life.

Therefore, move forward with confidence, seeking the tools and support you need. Anxiety may pose challenges, but it is also an opportunity to grow, learn, and flourish. Your journey towards a more balanced life, free from anxiety, begins now.

ABOUT THE AUTHOR

Leonardo Tavares carries within him not just the baggage of life, but also the wisdom garnered from confronting the tempests it has brought. A widower and devoted father to a charming young girl, he grasped that the journey of existence is a tapestry woven with highs and lows, a symphony of moments shaping our very essence.

With a vibrancy that transcends his youth, Leonardo has confronted challenges, navigated through arduous phases, and faced somber days. Despite pain having been a constant companion along his path, he metamorphosed these experiences into steps that propelled him to attain a plane of serenity and resilience.

The author of remarkable self-help works, including the books "Anxiety, Inc.", "Burnout Survivor", "Confronting the Abyss of Depression", "Discovering the Love of Your Life", "Facing Failure", "Healing the Codependency", "Rising Stronger", "Surviving Grief" and "What is My Purpose?", found in writing the medium to share his life lessons and convey the strength he unearthed within. Through his writing, clear and precise, Leonardo aids his readers in seeking strength, fortitude, and hope in times of profound sorrow.

Assist others by sharing his self-help works.

REFERENCES

Barlow, D. (2022). Anxiety: The Cognitive Behavioral Approach. New York, NY: The Guilford Press.

Bourne, E. J. (2022). Anxiety and Phobia Workbook. New York, NY: New Harbinger Publications.

Burns, D. (2022). When Panic Attacks: The New, Drug-Free Way to Overcome Panic Disorder and Anxiety. New York, NY: Houghton Mifflin Harcourt.

Goldin, P. R., & Gross, J. J. (2022). The Mindful Path to Self-Compassion: Freeing Yourself from Negative Thoughts and Emotions. New York, NY: Guilford Press.

Hofmann, S. G., & Smits, J. A. (2022). The Anxiety and Phobia Workbook: A Cognitive-Behavioral Therapy Approach to Overcoming Anxiety and Phobias. New York, NY: Guilford Press.

Leahy, R. L. (2022). The Worry Cure: Seven Steps to Stop Worrying and Start Living. New York, NY: Basic Books.

Levine, B. D. (2022). Anxiety Disorders: A Guide to Treatment and Prevention. New York, NY: W. W. Norton & Company.

Mcdonagh, B. (2022). The DARE Response: How to Overcome Anxiety, Panic, and Worry in 7 Weeks. New York, NY: New Harbinger Publications.

Weekes, C. (2022). Anxiety Toolkit: A Practical Guide for Managing Anxiety and Panic Attacks. New York, NY: HarperOne.

Williams, M., Penman, D., & Kabat-Zinn, J. (2022). Mindful Way Through Anxiety. New York, NY: The Guilford Press.

LEONARDO TAVARES

Anxiety, Inc.

www.ingramcontent.com/pod-product-compliance
Lightning Source LLC
LaVergne TN
LVHW041810060526
838201LV00046B/1205